This, my first book, is dedicated to my father
who taught me about honor and excellence
and who has never quite understood my
passion for the martial arts but
has always encouraged and
supported me nonetheless.

I would also like to dedicate this book to some great people who have helped me along the way. To Richard Fisher, who stuck by me through the worst of times. To my friend, James Jarrett, the last of a dying breed of samurai cowboys, a true master of weapons and tactics. To Bob Clapp, who taught me natural law and about strength in adversity. To Lance Clodfelter who has never once faltered in both friendship and loyalty. To Jeff Penrod and John White for their faith and dedication. To Ben Chen and Mitch Ives for their advice and counsel, and Mark Zbojniewicz for his support and encouragement. To William Becker, a lifelong martial artist and friend. To my very first student, David Bush, one of the finest police officers in the nation. Last but not least, to my good friend John Hutchison, a true warrior, and one of the few men whom I would trust to watch my back in a crisis.

I also want to express my gratitude to my students and instructors whom it has been my honor and pleasure to teach throughout the years. It has been said that to teach is to learn, and that has certainly been the case. A special thanks goes to Donna Clodfelter for editing this book and Amy Ng for her assistance in its production and design.

Thank you all.

TABLE OF CONTENTS

APPENDIXES

WARNING

The techniques, tactics, and methods described and depicted in this book are dangerous and should not be used or practiced in any way without extreme caution. The author and publisher will accept no responsibility, nor are they liable to any person or entity whatsoever for any injury, damage, or loss of any sort that may arise out of practicing, teaching, or disseminating of any of the techniques or ideas contained herein. This book is about an art form and should be viewed as such. This book is for *academic study only*.

PREFACE

I first met Richard Ryan the summer before my senior year of high school. I had been studying martial arts for some time and after talking with him, I became intrigued by his knowledge on the subject. In my first introduction to his art, he demonstrated a 1-inch punch on me that slammed into me with such incredible force that it sent me ten feet across the room. I had heard of the 1-inch punch that Bruce Lee had made famous, but I had never seen it, let alone had it performed on me with such dramatic effect. That started a student-teacher relationship and friendship that has spanned well over a decade.

Richard is a unique individual who possesses superior knowledge of martial arts and rare physical skills. His life has been spent in search of the truth and realities of combat, and he found them. He is the inventor of what is perhaps the most unique and practical martial arts system ever designed, the Dynamic Combat Method (DCM). A brutally effective, highly scientific system of personal survival, DCM is comprehensive in scope and devastating in application. As a four-limbed fighting system capable of blinding speed and bone crushing power, DCM is an art form based on science and reality, not theory and conjecture. Ryan is a master of both ancient and modern weaponry, and his specialty is the edged weapon for which his talents make him exceptionally deadly. Standing on the other end of his fists and feet is bad enough, but with an edged weapon he is truly frightening. I have witnessed firsthand his ability to cover a distance of eight feet and cut you half a dozen times in a blink of the

eye. But his genius really lies in his scientific methodologies that empower his art and the direct way in which he is able to present undeniable realities. He truly understands conflict and knows what it's like to fight for your life and what you need to survive. When it comes to learning to fight, he is exactly the type of person you want to listen to; one whose life has been immersed in the martial arts in every shape and form from the time he was a young boy.

The *Master of the Blade* is about the art of knife fighting. It is an informational and instructional manual for the use of the knife in combat and for self-defense. It provides priceless insights into a world shrouded in mystery, hype and mystique, and is perhaps the most comprehensive book ever written on the subject - certainly the most realistic. Ryan explores the art of the blade in a refreshing and often humorous manner presenting the stark realities of knife fighting in a way we can all understand and digest. The old adage "don't bring a knife to a gunfight" will not mean the same to you after reading this book.

Regardless of your level of knowledge and experience, you will learn more about real fighting in the short time that you read this book than you have probably learned in many years. May this experience enlighten you and bring you the confidence others have found in the study of the art of Dynamic Combat. Empty your cup, open your mind and enjoy.

Jeff Penrod
Dynamic Combat Senior Instructor
Former Police Officer

FOREWORD

Every civilization throughout history had a blade culture. Greece, Rome, India, China and Medieval Europe all revolved, to a various degree, around the use of the sword. In some cultures, skill with the edged weapon was elevated to the highest level of society such as in feudal Japan where the sword was literally worshiped. Until the middle 1800's, the entire Japanese culture focused on the warrior class and the use of the Katana. It was believed that the sword had a soul of its own, and the ability to use it was of such high social relevance it overshadowed almost everything else. Warriors were exalted to the highest levels of society.

Today we have an edged weapons subculture. The possession and use of knives are prevalent beneath the veneer of our more sophisticated society. Knives are legal and accessible. Anyone can go to the local mall or swap meet and buy the latest tactical folder and carry it without incident. People that cannot afford, purchase or carry a firearm can easily get an edged weapon. Most street people carry knives or razors of some kind. They are the easiest deadly weapon to acquire and perhaps the most misunderstood. Until now. The *Master of the Blade* takes you on a journey into the heart of one of the world's most effective personal survival tools. It provides a fresh look at a weapon that has been around since the dawn of time, and one that will exist as long as man rules this planet.

At first glance, this book seems to be a work of violence and destruction. Although it contains a prescription for violence, that's not what this book is about. Neither is it about killing, although many of the techniques are decidedly lethal. This book is about excellence. It's about personal development and self-confidence. It's about the kind of confidence that can only come from knowing that you can take care of yourself in the most extreme of situations. It's about the ability to use intelligence and cunning and the challenge of learning to deal with and survive one of the most primal and savage scenarios a human being can ever face, a life and death struggle with the blade.

The art of the blade is psychophysical art form, and a science that few people know and even fewer have ever mastered. It is art that unifies both mind and body by forging them into a weapon. A weapon that is not intended for malicious destruction but for self preservation. The edged weapon is an instrument of self reliance. But the true art of the blade is hard to find. Many of the books, videos and courses that teach "modern knife fighting" are impractical or incomplete, which makes them of little use for the serious student. I believe this book to be the most realistic and complete treatise on the art ever written. But it does not contain everything there is to know about knife fighting. No book can do that. Some things you cannot learn from the written word. This book does not even contain my entire system. What it does contain is the essence of the most effective and deadly knife fighting system in the world. Many concepts which could take entire chapters have been simplified and condensed to allow you to understand them quickly and bring them into play. Within these pages lie the secrets of the blade as an art form and as a weapon of war. You'll find it to be simple, realistic and brutally honest.

But I offer this warning. The knowledge contained herein is dangerous. I thought long and hard about publishing it, and I wish to express my concern about its nature. Even though some of the topics are approached with humor, this book is deadly serious, and this knowledge should not be taken lightly. Although the techniques and tactics can be lethal in application, this book is intended only as a scientific study of one of man's most misunderstood weapons. More importantly, it is not intended for children, but for the serious individual looking to improve his or her knowledge of martial arts and personal protection. Deal with the knowledge you acquire responsibly. Let honor and judgment guide your actions.

Richard Ryan
Blademaster

CHAPTER ONE

WEAPONS OF WAR

*"The ancient Romans built their greatest masterpieces
of architecture, the amphitheaters, for wild beasts and men to fight in."*

– Voltaire

Man is pathetic. When we compare ourselves to most animals, human beings are profoundly inferior. We are soft, fragile and easily injured. We lack a tough hide, thick fur or scales. We are bipeds, walking upright exposing our soft underbelly to attack. We don't have sharp claws or teeth, nor do we possess the strength of the elephant, the speed of the tiger or the agility of the ape. As a matter of fact, the average house cat is infinitely more prepared to survive than the average human being. Compared to most of our animal cousins, we are prey not predator. Physically, we belong on the low end of the food chain with the cattle and other livestock.

When man first appeared on this planet, he was little more than a walking sack of meat, providing other animals with a good meal and little danger of resistance. But we don't live in the kingdom of the animals anymore. We live in a world we have made. Eons later, this soft unimpressive mammal has become the master of the world. It is a world which we dominate completely and utterly. We have clawed our way to the top of the food chain to become the most dangerous and successful predator ever to roam the planet.

How did we do it? How did we come to dominate every other species on earth and shape the world in our own image? The answer is profoundly simple. Lacking the obvious physical gifts bestowed on other creatures, man had to adapt to survive. In order to hunt for food, defend himself and wage war, he had to find ways to overcome his deficiencies. He had to figure how to even the odds against him. Man became the supreme ruler of the world because of two things: intelligence and dexterity. For the first time in history, a creature emerged who could think with linear logic. Man was a being who could analyze, rationalize and invent without limit. He was an animal with an opposable thumb who could not only imagine but create. Intelligence, combined with an unprecedented physical dexterity, gave him the tools and weapons which mother nature did not. He developed tools that were harder, sharper and longer than his limbs. He developed implements he could use to fight and survive in a savage and hostile world. Man created weapons.

These weapons have been our obsession throughout our tenure on this planet. Perhaps no other single aspect of human life has so dominated our personal, social and political prosperity as the ability to make and

Time passed and man discovered metal. Copper and bronze were first used in southern Europe more than 6,000 years ago. This discovery changed forever the making of tools, weapons and the waging of war itself. Man formed the metal into countless variations of swords, daggers, knives, spears and axes. Around 600 B.C. man began crafting his weapons from iron. Weapons forged from iron and bronze reigned for centuries until the Middle Ages when steel was discovered. Steel, the strongest and most durable of the common metals, has remained the foundation on which all close combat weapons have been made up to the present day.

use weapons of war. Think about it. In ancient times, tools and weapons meant survival. They gave us the ability to hunt and kill and fend off other predators, whether on four legs or two. To an extent, the same is true today. Weapons or the threat of their deployment are still used to wage war, to maintain law and order and deter aggression. Above all else, weapons have kept us alive in a world in which we are physically inferior. Without them, we would have only been a footnote in the evolutionary chain.

THE CLAWS OF MAN

Early Paleolithic or Stone Age man discovered that if he chipped away at hard stones such as flint or obsidian, he could form them into pointed shapes. Such stones could be used for killing and skinning animals. They became the claws of man. Thousands of centuries later in the upper Paleolithic or later Stone Age, these stone tools became true weapons with the invention of the handle. Man learned to lash a handle of wood onto an ax or spear head and thereby took the first step toward centuries of weapon innovations to come.

Throughout mankind's existence the blade, particularly the sword, reigned as king. It has cut and slashed its way through history as man's weapon of choice. For tens of thousands of years, the edged weapon was the dominate survival tool and weapon of war. More people have died at the end of the sword than in all of our modern wars combined. This is true partly because of the simplicity and ease with which these weapons could be deployed. The sword is simple, swift, silent and deadly.

Parallel to the development of the sword was the creation of a shorter, more concealable weapon. Alongside the sword, the fighting knife has been part of man's arsenal since ancient times. These "short swords" took the form of daggers, knives and dirks and are carried in various forms throughout the world to this day. But the smaller blades of history never acquired the same mystique as their larger cousins, even though technically they are the oldest weapon in history. Stone knives were used over 500,000 years ago, but primarily as tools for skinning animals, cutting meat and scraping hides. The use of the knife in actual combat is a relatively recent development. The Stone Age was long gone before anything that might be described as a "fighting knife" appeared. The popularity of the knife has been overshadowed by other, more glamorous weapons. For example, the Roman war machine was driven by the short deadly sword called the Gladius, with the knife or dagger more or less consigned as a ceremonial weapon.

Nevertheless, the edged weapon, in the form of the sword, spear or dagger was the primary tool of war and self-defense for tens of thousands of years. Then, seemingly in the blink of an eye, it all changed. For untold centuries, with the exception of bows and throwing weapons, man had to stand toe-to-toe, look into eyes of another human being and take his life. Then man invented gunpowder. For the first time in history, the gun allowed a person to deliver death from a distance. Moreover, almost anyone could do it. You didn't have to be young, strong or skilled in the art of war, you just had to point and pull the trigger. From this point on, war began to evolve into the art of killing from a distance. The development of more efficient firearms gave way to bigger guns. Big guns and cannons gave way to bombs and missiles. The gun became so efficient that it has overshadowed all other weapons in history.

VIOLENCE AND SOCIETY

It is an unsettling truth that the entire history of mankind is written not by the pen, but with the sword. We have proven ourselves to be the most warlike and savage animal

on earth. Our history is drenched in blood. We claim to be more civilized and enlightened than our ancestors, but we are still the same old vicious predator. We look different. We may wear suits instead of animal skins, but our capacity for violence has remained with us as if it has been bred into our species.

You may argue that this is not the case, that today we have law and order and thus we are civilized. As a matter of fact, we have more laws today than any time in history. But the truth is that we have a semblance of law and order. Laws have done little to stop or curb the flow of blood in our society. Beneath the veneer of our civilized world lies the constant specter of violence. It's just less visible than in centuries past. Hordes of bandits don't come swooping down from the hills on a regular basis. Tanks don't roam our streets, at least not where I live. But crime and violence do permeate our inner cities and it's a good bet that there is, at very least, one war going on somewhere in the world right now as you read this book.

Everyday people from all walks of life are assaulted, attacked or killed, and not by beasts of prey, but by other people just like themselves. They are not killed for food, or as a part of natural selection, but for reasons our animal cousins would never comprehend. Man is the only animal that kills for reasons other than survival. We are the ultimate predator because we kill for so many diverse reasons. Just pick one - love, money, revenge, greed, jealousy, hate, fear, even fun.

We are violent. You need only check out the daily newspaper or turn on the evening news to know this is true. Everyday almost everywhere someone is beaten, shot, stabbed or killed for the most stupid of reasons. These are not anomalies. This is the status quo. When you remember that what reaches the news constitutes only the most sensational and newsworthy stories, you begin to see the true picture. The potential for violent conflict entering our lives exists each and every day. It is part of the realities of our world. It could come from a mugger, a rapist, a robber, an acquaintance, a stranger or even a family member. It could happen anytime, anywhere and to anyone. No one is immune to its touch. This, above all else, is why you should study self defense and weaponcraft. It is your inalienable right to live your life free from harm and to protect the ones you love. This book is a text on knife fighting, but even more fundamentally, it is about being smart. My purpose is to provide you with the information you need to learn how to use one of man's most efficient and devastating self defense tools. It is a tool that you can learn with relative ease, and one that you can carry with you almost anywhere. This tool

doesn't jam or run out of ammunition and it is one that someday could save your life.

THE ART OF KNIFE FIGHTING

The art of knife fighting has been, for the most part, an endeavor shrouded in mystery and misconception. When compared to all that has been said and written about the sword arts of European fencing or Japanese Kendo, realistic information on knife fighting is almost nonexistent. The first written manual to discuss knife fighting as a combative art form was written in 1849 by a man known only as M. D. R. Although this man has been swallowed by history, it is likely that he was a disinherited Spanish or Italian aristocrat. The manual was aimed at the "common man" with the author making frequent derogatory comments about the "so-called decent class." The book focused on a specific knife called the Navaja, a Spanish clasp knife dating back to the late 15th century. It was the forerunner of the modern switchblade or "flick knife" with a slightly oval blade folding into the handle. Versions of the blade are still used throughout the Spanish speaking world. Because of its design, the Navaja was usually used to slash at an opponent and much of the text focuses on this skill. Other than that, there are very few texts that were ever written on the knife before the mid twentieth century. This is partially due to the fact that the art of knife fighting has never been studied as in individual and complete science unto itself. In ages past, there were so many other options if you got into a fight, the knife or dagger was usually a weapon of last resort or of assassination. So many other types of weapons were plentiful. They were part of everyday life in almost every corner of the world. In the past, people were free to carry any weapon they wanted to. Why would you use a nine inch dagger when you've got a 72 inch broadsword strapped to your hip? It was a simple matter of

In an age overrun by technology, the knife offers a simple and deadly contrast to man's modern weapons of mass destruction. More than just a throwback to ancient times, the edged weapon has found a new home in today's society where gun laws choke away our rights to bear arms. Moreover, this ancient tool has found a new life in the bosom of technology, reborn as the modern tactical folder. A new industry has taken roots and the blade has found itself more prolific than ever. To most, the knife is still a tool. We use it to cut our steaks and open our mail. But this seemingly benign tool is also a deadly weapon that anyone can carry. In its incarnation as a folding or pocket knife, it has become a socially accepted accessory. Everyone seems to be carrying a knife these days, from the banker to the construction worker to the housewife, they are everywhere. Yet only the smallest fraction of these people have even the vaguest idea of how to use it for what it was originally intended. The knife is more than just a tool. It is the ultimate close quarter survival weapon. But to use it effectively requires an uncommon knowledge based on reality, not fantasy or theory. This is knowledge you will find in this book, the *Master of the Blade*.

firepower. But modern times brought modern laws and throughout much of the world it became illegal to carry and display obviously deadly weapons. With this dramatic social shift, the knife, with its ability to be easily concealed, became a more obvious choice for personal defense.

Much of the true art and science of knife fighting, if it ever really existed, has been lost in the sands of time. Those skilled in the art of the knife rarely shared their insights and many probably took their knowledge with them to the grave. Though some knowledge has survived the ages, much of it is based on European or Asian sword fighting systems. Even today in the age of mass media, there are few worthwhile texts written on the edged weapon.

CHAPTER TWO

DYNAMIC COMBAT

"Power is knowledge applied."

– Richard Ryan

Most martial arts schools focus almost exclusively on unarmed combat skills. Most teach kicks, punches and throws, but not how to use a knife, stick or firearm. In ancient times, weapons sets were much more important than unarmed training. Why would you use your hands when weapons were all around you and carried freely? It's only with the modern commercialization of karate schools that serious weapons training has been edited from the curriculums. But weapons have always been an integral part of the arts of war. If your goal is realistic self-defense training and the art you are studying does not teach and emphasize the use of modern weapons, go elsewhere.

This book is about blade combat. More specifically, it is about my Tactical Edged Weapons system. This is a system of knife fighting that stems from the martial art of DCM (the Dynamic Combat Method). As an art, Dynamic Combat encompasses the entire spectrum of human conflict from verbal self defense and confrontation management skills to the control or destruction of attackers in both armed and unarmed situations. But one of the most interesting features of

Dynamic Combat is its weaponcraft. Few martial arts in the world can boast a range of weapons as varied as DCM. From environmental weapons such as rocks, pencils, bottles, combs and ash trays to the modern handgun, shotgun and the assault rifle, Dynamic Combat addresses every combative tool available today. They are all treated equally under the system. Even the use of expedient weapons such as a pen or chair is taught with the same scientific tactics as the knife, baton and handgun.

Since the tactical edged weapons system in this book originates from a specific combat art, it is important to delve at least briefly into some of the essential principles on which the mother system is based. These principles are the cornerstones of the art. They lay a foundation of reality and help you better understand the general philosophies, techniques and tactics to follow.

THE END RESULT THEORY

The end result theory is the most important and fundamental concept in DCM. It permeates every aspect of the system. It states that in any situation the most important thing is that you walk away alive.

The single most important goal is your survival. The exact techniques and methods you use to achieve this goal are secondary concerns. What matters is that you walk away alive or you protect the innocent life of someone else. Therefore everything you learn and do should be directed toward this premise. All techniques and tactics must be based on reality. They must be effective when it counts. Anything that is not immediately effective is useless and should be discarded from your survival plan.

TOTAL APPROACH THEORY

In combat no single weapon or technique is superior to all others. Superiority depends on the person and his use of techniques and tactics. For example, in a elevator, close range strikes and grappling defenses work well. In a parking lot, kicks and punches might be better. It all depends on your immediate needs. Therefore, to be effective you should learn a wide variety of practical skills. The total approach concept implies that combat is fundamentally unpredictable and because of this, you need a wide variety of skill sets to survive. If you want to be truly safe in a hostile world, you should explore all areas of personal protection. Explore as many skill sets as possible. The master fighter has no prejudices. He does not exclude any technique, method or tactic as long as it is firmly grounded in reality. For example, you should treat biting and clawing tactics with the same science as kicking and punching. The master uses all ways as means to the end.

Although this book is predominately about the edged weapon, many of the techniques and concepts will carry over to other aspects of combat as well. There are certain techniques and concepts that are critical to your ability to use what is written in this book. First, you must have a crystal clear understanding of the realities of the use of the blade itself. The edged weapon is a tool.

As such, it must be used in a specific way in order to be effective. Violate the rules of use and its effectiveness is negated. Knowing your tools is the first commandment. A worker doesn't show up on a construction site not knowing how to use his saw or hammer. Understanding what works and what doesn't is your first job. You must also understand under what conditions you cannot use the blade. Ignoring the law is the surest way to end up in prison. The blade is considered a deadly weapon and, as such, its use is restricted to specific situations.

WORST CASE SCENARIOS

In addition to having a total approach to fighting, you need methods to deal with worst case scenarios. If you are going to rely on the edged weapon as a self defense tool, you want to train to deal with the absolute worst situation you'll ever come across. All of your training, even the basics, should be focused on surviving the most savage and brutal scenario you might face. In other words, learn the basics, then learn to deal with the worst that may happen to you. This is the overload principle. If I can teach you to survive one round with Mike Tyson, teaching you how to evade, grab, strike, bite and gouge your way through three brutal minutes and survive, then everyone else you might actually face in your life will be considerably easier to deal with. If your training has provided you with the ability to deal with the most dangerous situation and people you ever may come across, you have considerable leeway in the use of force. Highly skilled fighters don't have to use all their skills in a fight against an inferior opponent, but the reverse is not true. If you don't acquire the skill to deal with the worst case scenario, then you will likely overreact and you may hurt someone who doesn't

need to be hurt. This being the case, much of this manual is devoted to the skills needed to deal with another human being, standing in front of you, who also knows how to use the knife. That's the worst case scenario for the blade. If I can teach you how to deal with someone with a blade, the guy with the tire iron or pool que will be easy.

These three DCM concepts are the key elements that set the stage for what is to come. The end result theory prepares us for the idea that we will do whatever we must to survive, while the total approach theory allows us the freedom to explore any and all ways of achieving this goal. In training, the focus on the development of skills to survive the worst case scenario ensures us that we will learn to deal with the greatest threat we may face. Such extreme training creates the freedom to respond with lesser force when appropriate to do so.

CHAPTER THREE

THE REAL WORLD

*"An understanding of reality is essential in the search for truth.
If you don't acknowledge reality, it automatically works against you."*

– Richard Ryan

I realize that I may offend some people with some of the things I say in this chapter. But I made a promise to myself a long time ago that I would tell the truth no matter what it is. I have spent my life in a search for the truth of combat and to alter it for the sake of placating egos is the ultimate sell out. To learn the art of war, you must first start with the truth. In war there is no place for ignorance or self deception. An axiom I live by is, "If you don't acknowledge reality, it will automatically work against you." Reality is what is. It is not open to interpretation and it is not negotiable. A student of self-defense must embrace realities of combat no matter what they are. This being said, I offer a preemptive apology to those whom I may offend. But truth is the basis for all knowledge.

A REALITY CHECK

In the past, fighting was a practical life skill. Considering all the perils that one may have faced back then on a daily basis, self preservation skills were an absolute necessity. With the advance of civilization came law and order. Well, at least some degree of law and order. Swords and spears were laid to rest in favor of plow shears and farm tools. Man became civilized. Today Ming the merciless does not roam the hills ready to swoop down and take your possessions or your life. Most of us do not wake up with the fear of having to fight for our life everyday. This social order has led to the proliferation of both practical and impractical fighting arts. Today there are more martial arts styles than in any time in history. From a practical standpoint, some of these styles are good. Some are great. And some will just plain get you killed.

The point I'm trying to make is that, unlike the past, reality does not necessarily have to be an ingredient in today's martial arts. Both styles and instructors don't have to be realistic to be successful. They just have to look good and have good marketing. You can build an expensive looking and beautiful house on dirt and from the outside it will look like any other home, but it's still built on dirt. It will crumble with the first real storm. Today, most martial artists, firearms aficionados, and knife fighting instructors don't have to worry about actually testing their skills on the battlefield. They don't have to worry that if their techniques don't work they'd be dead. Only a fraction of the people who teach martial arts and self defense have ever been in a real fight in their life. And a fraction of a fraction of those who teach knife fighting have ever been in a fight with a blade. On top of that, few of them are willing to put on the gear and spar full contact to test their ability. But they still teach. This is similar to taking swimming lessons from an instructor who has never actually been in the water. If you are going to teach fighting, you have to fight. At very least, you have to put in the hours sparring and testing your skills under realistic conditions. There is no substitute for battle. Even with reality-based sparring, you can only come close to reality. It's still not the same as facing another human being bent on your destruction. This is the root of much of the problems with martial arts and weapons training today. Theories and styles abound, and most people cannot tell whether or not a person or a style is truly effective. Just because someone can spew forth theories ad nauseum doesn't make him a fighter. There are many people who write extensively about the combative use of guns, knives and martial arts techniques who wouldn't last two seconds in a real fight.

How do you determine if someone is for real? Well, that can be difficult. They may look like a duck, talk like a duck and walk like a duck, but they are actually turkeys. The best way is to test them. Acquire some knowledge on the subject, then ask technical questions and listen carefully to the answers. Do they make sense? Are they realistic and practical? Better yet, watch the person in action or do what I do, ask him to spar with you. If you're not up to it, ask if you can watch him spar one of his top students. This should give you an indication of his true level of skill.

WRITERS NOT FIGHTERS

If I haven't offended someone already I'm sure I will with this next section. But

remember that I don't consider reality negotiable. Many of the people who write for the martial arts, gun and knife magazines are writers, not fighters. They pontificate endlessly about this technique or that technique, or the design of this weapon versus that one. Often they discuss things that have little to do with the real world. They demonstrate an endless array of sanitized techniques that would only work against the most inept of attackers. Martial arts, knife and gun magazines are great. They present new ideas and give you an idea of what's out there. But they shouldn't be the source of your knowledge about combat. Remember that they are a business and, as such, present all aspects of the arts without a lot of scrutiny. When you see an article about fighting, study the text and pictures. Imagine what would happen if the techniques illustrated were used at full speed against a resistant opponent. Or better still, take a black marker and draw in an effective guard stance on the guy being demonstrated upon. Inevitably 90 percent of the techniques illustrated would be thwarted in some way.

MAKERS AND FAKERS

I have one more area to address that is very relevant to the knife industry. There are a lot of great knife makers out there. Some are consummate artists. They design and make things out of steel that have incredible beauty and craftsmanship. However, just because someone is a knife maker, (even a famous one), does not automatically qualify him to teach knife combat. The designer of the Glock pistol was an engineer, not a combat firearms instructor. He created a great firearm but didn't teach how to use it. But for some reason, some people who make knives suddenly transform into masters of the blade. Knowing about knife technology and using knives in combat are two distinctly different things. Knife makers are often highly skilled craftsmen, but that skill seldom translates to combat ability. The point is, if you are going to learn about something as brutal and final as combat, you'd better learn it from someone who knows the realities and has the skills to prove it.

STYLES AND SYSTEMS

Martial arts are 80 percent baloney. That's right, when it comes to real fighting, when it comes to a knock down, drag-out bite-your-face-off, do anything-to-survive encounter with a highly motivated attacker, most martial arts systems and techniques are predominately useless. Yet they prosper. Self defense is big business, and business is good. There are a lot of styles out there. Most are limited in scope and application. Often, they focus on one specific technique or tactic. For example, some knife fighting systems gear their entire training toward the fixed blade, or techniques that use a specific grip or striking method. I know of a celebrated knife fighting teacher who teaches only quick draw tactics with the ice pick grip. He shows you how fast you can draw a blade from a scabbard at your belt and pop a balloon at close range. At first glance, it can be rather impressive. But as far as I know, no one was ever killed by a balloon. They don't move, slash, stab, or counterstrike. Skill at drawing quickly from the scabbard and popping a balloon will not impress a seasoned knife fighter who will not let you get close enough to do so without escape or retaliation.

What's more, there are legal problems with quick draw attacks, let alone the idea of carrying a fixed blade knife in a sheath designed for immediate use. You had better be prepared to explain why you carry such a weapon in everyday life. The average person doesn't carry a fixed blade combat fighting knife in a sheath designed for quick draw. If you use this system, it had better be in a obvious life and death encounter, and if you survive you'll still have some explaining to do. If you're not careful you could find yourself living behind concrete and steel. I am not saying that such techniques are wholly invalid, only that they are restrictive in nature. We deploy similar techniques in my art, but only under specific tactical conditions. To build an entire system around a limited series of techniques and tactics is foolish.

I made the statement that martial arts are 80 percent baloney. Unfortunately this is true. Having said this, I do want to present the whole story. The other side of the story is that the remaining 20 percent of martial arts and weapons training comprises the most impressive, most dangerous and effective techniques and tactics for survival man has ever devised. There seems to be no gray area. Bad martial arts are really bad and the good ones are really great. Part of the reason this is true today is that we live in the information age. Mass communication has brought the free exchange of ideas. Centuries ago, a martial arts master seldom came across another stylist with radically different techniques from his own. Today there is the greatest exchange of ideas and information the world has ever seen and it has allowed for the proliferation of the good as well as the bad. As a result, the reality-based systems, instructors (and writers) out there have benefited from this proliferation of ideas and have gotten even better. Although they represent only a small fraction of the people and systems out there, they are without a doubt the best of the best. The bottom line is that there is a lot of baloney out there. Some of it is disguised or packaged to look and smell good but it's still baloney. If you want to know the truth of combat and you want to acquire real skill, skill that you could bet your life on, you need to develop your bullshit detection meter.

What then constitutes a reality-based combat system? What are the ingredients you need to look for in an art you may have to bet your life on? Following is a brief description of the attributes of a reality-based combat system.

GROSS MOTOR SKILLS

A fighting art must be more than a collection of lethal moves. Although such techniques should comprise the core of the art, there are many more things that must be considered. On a technical level, it must be easy to learn and apply. But more importantly, the primary techniques must be based on gross motor skills. Extremely complex techniques will put you in the grave when all hell breaks loose. This is because when we are thrust into situations of high stress, most of our fine motor skills go out the window. When a person's heart rate reaches 160-180 beats per minute or more, the neural system is incapable of performing finite actions. Apply this truth to the knife and you begin to realize that all those intricate cut and trapping

actions performed in class with such precision disappear under great duress. Under high stress you will revert to simple gross actions.

I was invited to a martial arts tournament years ago to give a demonstration of Dynamic Combat. There I met an instructor who taught, and I quote, "the worlds deadliest combat karate system." On his uniform in blood red letters was written "Combat Karate... One Shot Knockout!" He boasted to me about how he could hit a man just right, in the exact spot and render him instantly unconscious. "Wow, I have to see this," I told him. He was a big heavyweight and when his bout came, he strutted into the ring confident that he would finish his opponent quickly. Well, I guess it didn't happen as he expected. By the third round both fighters were standing toe-to-toe in the center of the ring, arms flailing away like windmills smacking each other solidly in the head. The only effect was the look of exhaustion and exasperation on their faces. The point is that if you base all your skills on extreme precision or complexity, you'd better hope you can end the fight really quickly before your heart rate gets you in trouble. Precise actions and techniques are fine for the beginning of a situation or for the highly conditioned fighter whose conditioning will not allow his blood pressure to rise too high. If this is you, never mind. If not, the core techniques of your art should be based on simple motor skills you can deploy even under great duress.

GENERIC BASICS

Next, the basic tactics of a combat art must allow for as many situations as possible. You never know how or where violence will go down. If you limit your tactics, you limit your responses. Let's say you've spent the last 20 years studying Tae Kwon-do (TKD) . For those of you that don't know, Tae Kwon-do is a style of martial arts developed in the rolling hills of Korea which emphasizes the use of long range kicking techniques. The art was developed in open space, not urban sprawl. When you have space, kicking can be effective. Many people are attracted to it because the kicking techniques resemble what they see in the movies. It is arguably the most popular martial art in the world today because of this fact. Let's say you're a black belt TKD instructor. You can do the full splits. You can kick apples off of a guy's head. You have won tournaments, and you spar with your classmates all the time. Great. One day, you stop at a pay phone to call your girlfriend. You enter the booth, slide a quarter in the slot and snap, click, some street thug grabs you, shoves you up against the wall and sticks a switchblade in your face. Try doing a jump spinning back kick in a phone booth. Even if you know what to do, you will hesitate because the basic techniques of the art that you studied are based on an extreme - the extreme of long range kicking.

In the same way, a combat art must emphasize basics that are neutral, meaning the techniques must be generic enough to handle a wide variety of situations and attackers. With functional generic techniques as a foundation, you can always expand to secondary options when it becomes advantageous to do so.

ADVANCED TECHNIQUES

This brings us to the third attribute of a combat art. As much as the basics must be simple and generic, it should have a reservoir of advanced techniques, tactics and strategies to cope with unusual or extreme situations. There are times when even the most generic and simple basics will be ineffective and you must resort to more advanced maneuvers to save your life. The system should allow you the capability of fighting in that phone booth or parking lot

or wherever. It should be able to deal with all other forms of weaponry and handle multiple threats. It should provide the advanced student with strategies for defeating specific types of fighters and provide answers to advanced tactical problems. In short, the basics should be devastatingly easy and effective and, like the tip of the iceberg, should only be a hint of its depth of knowledge.

LEGAL AND MORAL ISSUES

We live in a society of laws. Break them and you face the consequences. Use force when you shouldn't, or use excessive force, and you may find yourself living with the very people you were trying to defend against. You have every right to defend yourself or your loved ones, but only to the extent that it remains an act of self defense. Along with your practical survival skills, you have to learn about and abide by the law. Too many teachers provide their students with potentially lethal tactics without even a word about the consequences of irresponsible use of such techniques. With power comes responsibility. The knife is a deadly weapon. Learn how to use it and you become the deadly weapon. You must know when, how and to what limit you are capable of using such power.

THINGS TO LOOK FOR IN A COMBAT MARTIAL ART

1. Techniques and tactics must be reality-based and easy to learn and apply.
2. The system must be vast in scope. The system must be comprised of beginning, advanced and master level techniques.
3. It must deal with the legal/moral aspects of the use of force.
4. It must provide comprehensive physiological and psychological training.
5. It must deal with worst case scenarios.
6. It must provide comprehensive training in both armed and unarmed combat.

STYLES AND SYSTEMS TO AVOID

1. Complex or fancy arts resembling what you see in the movies.
2. Systems that focus on one technique, type of weapon or tactic without any tactical depth.
3. Systems that provide no legal, moral or psychological training.
4. Systems that deal in only the best case situations instead of the worst case scenario.

CHAPTER FOUR

THE EDGE OF REALITY

"If you aren't quick, you might be dead."

– Richard Ryan

This chapter is about the realities of the blade. It's about what happens when you find yourself in a real fight, in which knives are involved. I thought about starting this section by talking about how swift, fast and deadly the edged weapon can be and how few people are prepared to deal with it. We could talk about how most people underestimate the speed of an attack with a knife, and how they just seem to stand there like a deer caught in the headlights. But all these things will become clear to you soon enough. I thought about telling you some war stories about the situations I have been in, in which weapons were involved. But alas, they would be very short stories. Most of the fights I have experienced in my life have been over almost as soon as they have begun. Having learned early on that speed was the most important ingredient to victory, I have used it to overwhelm almost all my opponents in seconds. Most of the fights I have been in have been sudden and brutal. You would learn little from most of these stories. But there is one fight with the blade that stands out above all others. I decided to start this chapter by relaying the story of the first time I was attacked by someone with a knife because, in the end, I learned more about the realities

of the blade in this single situation than in any other I have been in since.

ATTACKED WITH THE BLADE

When I was younger I had a girlfriend who had just broken up with a guy a few months earlier. I won't bore you with the details, but the guy had a reputation of being a punk, which was one of the reasons she left him. He didn't take it well. Weeks passed and he was more or less stalking her. After one episode which left her shaking and in tears, I went to confront him. I found him sitting in his garage at a work bench fiddling with a carburetor. He glanced at me once, as I walked up, and never once looked at me again. He just kept working silently which I've got to admit was a little unnerving. Angered, I got right up in his face and told him in no uncertain terms that she didn't want to see him again, and that from now on he was going to leave her alone. He never said anything. I forcefully repeated myself with no response. He just stared straight ahead at the wall. In hindsight, I later grew to recognize this response as the "thousand yard stare," one of the reactions some people have to a threat and often a preparation for a surprise attack. I asked him if he heard me.

Again there was no response, so I repeated myself one last time. As I turned to leave, I caught a glimpse of motion out of the corner of my eye. A blur was streaking toward my lower back. It happened so fast, I didn't really know what he was trying to do, but I knew it was hostile.

Without thinking I deflected the attack, spun around and struck him solid in the face with a backhand. My fists slammed into his face a half a dozen times in the few seconds that followed. A front stomp kick to the stomach catapulted him back into the table, knocking him over his chair. He slumped to the ground with a dull thud. I flew at him poised to strike again, but he was out of it. Blood flowed from his face. His nose looked like it was hit by a sledge hammer and was split right down the middle. Both eyes were beginning to swell shut and his upper lip was split to the teeth. I grabbed him by the hair and cocked my fist to strike him again, but his eyes were rolled up into his head. I let him drop back to the floor.

As he fell I glanced at an old Buck hunting knife which had fallen from his grasp. When I saw it, my heart began to race. It was then I noticed that my sweat shirt was covered in blood on the right side of my body. My blood. "He stabbed me." I thought to myself, "I can't believe he stabbed me," Feverishly I checked my torso looking for wounds. Then I saw it. The blood came not from my body, but from a wound in my arm. I had deflected

the attack on my torso, but apparently didn't get my other arm out of the way in time. He had stabbed me deeply, but I barely felt it as blood pumped from the wound. Anger swelled up in me again. I was furious because he had attacked me from behind like a coward. He moaned in the corner as he tried to get up. I kicked the knife away and it hit the far wall with a clang. I wish I could tell you that I didn't hit him again, but I did - a side kick to his chest sending him slamming into the corner and slumping back down to the floor. Today I probably wouldn't have struck him again, but I was young and hot headed back then. Although he was semi-conscious, I grabbed him and told him in no uncertain terms that if he ever harassed me or my girlfriend again I would kill him. I don't know if he heard me but I know he got the point.

I wrapped my arm in my shirt and drove myself to the hospital. I remember that I never felt the wound until it began to throb. Then the pain came. It had been masked by adrenaline, which was an important lesson unto itself. As it turned out, I deflected the knife away from my back but the knife buried itself in the bone of my upper forearm. I decided to tell the doctor I had slipped and cut myself with a kitchen knife.

I know he didn't believe me but he didn't press it. While I sat there getting sutured, I thought about pressing charges, but it was just the two of us in the garage and he could just as easily say that I attacked him. I decided to let it go. In retrospect that was stupid. I should have called the police. As it turns out, neither I nor my girlfriend ever saw him again.

The encounter remained in my thoughts for a long time. Had I not been studying martial arts, I could have been killed that day. It was the quick reactions I had developed that had saved my life. I had also realized some important insights that I will pass on to you.

First, the edged weapon is a great equalizer. This guy was no match for me physically and he knew it. But by picking up a simple tool, he became more than my equal. In one action he went from homosapien to homosuperior. He grabbed a steel claw to fight with. In one shot he could have killed me with it; something he could never have accomplished with his empty hands. I think that fits the definition of a great equalizer, and it began to spark my interest in the use and defense of all weapons, especially the blade.

Second, never underestimate how fast someone can attack you. When motivated, people can explode on you in a fraction of a second. Never ever take your eyes off an attacker even for an instant. The attack had been swift enough without my turning my back on him. This was an amateur's mistake. Remember that people are wholly unpredictable. You never know what a person will do, and when a conflict or argument arises, it is a good idea to always expect to be attacked. Before that night the last thing I expected was for this punk to actually try to kill me over the situation. From that day forward, I never underestimated anyone, and no one has ever

gotten the drop on me since. I began to expect the unexpected, and you should too.

Third, I learned that even with a technical advantage like a blade, victory often goes to the swiftest. He who hits first, fastest and the most almost always wins. He didn't expect me to instantly respond with a vicious counterattack. He probably thought he would bury the knife in my back and gloat. It still makes me mad. The point is that even though the knife is a great weapon, it's not the weapon that counts, it's you. Always remember that any weapon is just a tool. The mind controls the body and the body controls the tools. A fighter must develop himself first. You must become the weapon before you use one. When you are the weapon, the tools of combat, whether knife, stick, gun or rock are easy to deploy. Conversely, without the proper knowledge and training, the greatest weapon on earth might not save you in a crisis. Knowledge is power. Perhaps more correctly, knowledge is potential power. Knowledge applied is the ultimate power.

In the end, my first experience at being attacked by someone with a knife was a good one. My injury, the price of admission, was a small price to pay for the knowledge I gained. It was a lesson in reality and the experience changed my thinking and sparked my interest in the use and defense of the edged weapon.

It is imperative for you to understand the edged weapon. Reality must permeate everything you do from here on out. Without this sober clarity, you risk your life more than you have to. Most people underestimate what an edged weapon can do. People get killed all the time by a great assortment of pointed or sharp objects. Some people are killed almost instantly, while for others death comes more slowly. The lucky ones are only maimed for life, left with the telltale signs of their encounter. My body carries quite a few scars as a reminder of my experiences. The edged weapon is one of the most efficient killing tools man has ever devised. In close combat, it has more advantages and less disadvantages than any other weapon.

THE ADVANTAGES OF THE EDGED WEAPON

We have discussed the history of the blade from its conception as a tool to its use in war. We have examined the realities of both combat martial arts and the edged weapon itself. We have determined what constitutes an effective defensive system and what you should avoid. It's time to begin to address the blade from a technical point of view. We start by analyzing the specific advantages and disadvantages of the edged weapon as a defensive tool.

THE TOUCH WEAPON

First and foremost, the greatest advantage of the edged weapon is that it need only touch you to cause damage. Contact usually means cutting. Unlike your fists, feet or impact tools, a small child could injure or kill you with a razor blade. Strength and power are an advantage in any confrontation, but of much lesser consequence in a knife fight. The edged weapon requires very little speed and even less strength to do its job. Accuracy and precision are far more important than brute strength. Like the firearm, it can be carried and used regardless of age and physical condition. Moreover, in the hands of a fast, strong athlete, the edged weapon can be immensely frightening.

A MULTIDIRECTIONAL TOOL

Another advantage of the edged weapon is the fact that it can come at you from any conceivable angle and still be effective. Unarmed combat skills require exact body mechanics. You have to do things correctly to be effective. In martial arts, each individual punch or kick has its own set of technical guidelines. Ignore body mechanics and you become miserably ineffective. In addition, the most fundamental functional skill of unarmed combat is the control and maintenance of balance. You must maintain balance to be effective. Lose it and even the biggest, strongest and most skilled become functionally weak. This is not true for the edged weapon. You need neither perfect balance nor exact body mechanics to strike effectively with the blade. You could be bent over the hood of a car, on the ground being strangled, in a headlock or any number of unfortunate positions and if you can get to your knife, you can hurt or kill the attacker with ease.

THE PSYCHOLOGICAL EDGE

The edged weapon has a unique psychological advantage. It represents a primal fear. The fear of being torn open, cut or eaten has transcended time and manifested itself as a respect for sharp objects. To test this, take out a razor sharp

One major advantage of the edged weapon is that it can be deployed from virtually any angle.

tactical knife and hand it to almost anyone and watch his reaction. Most people will acknowledge a very healthy respect and some will exhibit something resembling a phobia. Sharp objects can be scary because we innately know what they could do to us. In a fight, this can give you an advantage that most other weapons don't have. Most sane people will run when faced with the prospect of being cut or stabbed. Although you should never anticipate it, some people will flee when you display an edged weapon, especially if it looks like you know exactly how to use it.

DISADVANTAGES OF THE EDGED WEAPON

Technically the edged weapon has no distinct disadvantages. The only disadvantages it has are the disadvantages of any and all weapons, not just the knife. The first disadvantage is the fact that it is a weapon. As a tool separate form your body, to be of use you must have it with you at the time of need. Murphy's Law tells us that the time that you leave the tool on the dresser to go to the store for a quart of milk is the time you'll probably need it.

MYTHS OF KNIFE COMBAT

I'll end this chapter with a general discussion of the common myths that surround the edged weapon today. Myths are untruths and without the truth you have no chance against someone who abides by it. Myths give birth to unrealistic techniques and tactics. Remember my rule, "If you don't acknowledge reality, it will automatically work against you." Here are some of the most common myths and the truths that follow them.

MYTH: The edged weapon is the ultimate survival tool.

REALITY: The ultimate survival tool is you. Tools are useless unless directed correctly. If you are the weapon, then almost any tool will do. A pencil in the hands of a combat master is much more deadly than the most lethal fighting knife in the hands of a unskilled and unwilling novice. The mind controls the body and the body controls the tools. If you are unable, or unwilling to use any weapon, that weapon is useless. You are the weapon, and you hone the weapon with knowledge, practice and experience.

TRUTH: Every weapon is just an extension of the mind and body. The ultimate weapon is you.

MYTH: Knife fighting requires years of dedicated training.

Reality: Mastering the art of the blade does require a great deal of time and experience. But you don't have to master it to use it. Because the blade is a touch weapon, it does not necessarily require any special degree of physical prowess. Almost anyone can learn the basics in a few short hours. Once the basics are learned, everything you learn from that point on becomes an even greater advantage.

TRUTH: The basics of a good knife fighting system can be learned in a very short time frame.

MYTH: Knives are useless against a gun.

REALITY: In the right hands, edged weapons are a devastating close quarter battle tool. But to be effective, they require close proximity. Statistically most fights (armed or unarmed) occur at conversational distance. At this range, a skilled individual with a knife can kill you in a matter of seconds with a swarm of steel. He can trap, grab and deflect the firearm and render it useless. On the other hand, if the fighter with the gun can create and maintain distance or provide some type of barrier, it is he who has the advantage.

TRUTH: Which weapon has the advantage is a matter of tactical logistics. Under certain conditions, a knife can be more lethal than a firearm and vice versa.

MYTH: Ferocious looking "Rambo-like knives" will intimidate an attacker.

REALITY: In a conflict, the level of intimidation and fear someone may feel is always an unknown. Whether or not someone is intimidated usually has little to do with the weapon and everything to do with the person wielding it. You cannot intimidate someone who is not intimidatable. Any weapon, no matter how fierce looking, is just a weapon. The real threat comes from the person behind it. A butter knife in the hands of a person who moves and acts like he knows exactly how to use it can be just as frightening.

TRUTH: Never assume that you can intimidate anyone with any weapon.

MYTH: All knife fighting styles are basically the same.

REALITY: If being the same means they all use a knife, then I guess they are all similar. But that's like saying all computers are the same. They may look similar on the outside, but it is what is on the inside that counts. How fast are they? How easy are they to learn? How efficient? How outdated? Although all systems have some value, some are good, some better and a few, the best.

TRUTH: Not all systems are created equal. Some are more efficient, comprehensive and more user friendly than others.

MYTH: Throwing your knife can be a good self-defense technique.

REALITY: Would you throw your loaded handgun at an attacker? Why throw away a perfectly good weapon? Even the most skilled knife thrower cannot easily peg a quick moving target, especially if that target is flying at him with fists, feet or weapons of his own. Throwing knives can be a fun past time, but it has no place in combat. Leave it to the sideshows and carnivals.

TRUTH: Throwing knives is not an effective use of the knife. Get a spear.

MYTH: Knife fighting is very common in the streets.

REALITY: Although not unheard of, knife fighting, especially the duels like we see in the movies, is not a common occurrence. When you think about it, there are so many other possible scenarios. Dynamic Combat defines five forms of weapons: edged, impact, flexible, ballistic and combinations. Each of these weapons categories has almost infinite variations on the theme. Lump all forms of unarmed combat into one broad category and you've got six general scenarios involving methods of attack. Not withstanding people's preferences toward the use of a particular weapon like the handgun, you've still got an average probability curve of one in six or 16.6 percent chance of an attack with an edged weapon.

TRUTH: Statistically, you've got less than a one in six chance of facing a blade in a real encounter.

MYTH: Slashes are better than stabs or vice versa.

REALITY: Is it better to be shot or run through with a sword? Is it better to have your throat cut or hit in the head with a baseball bat? Obviously neither is preferable. The worst attack is the one that gets you. Depending on where and how you are struck, any attack by any weapon could be the worst one. The idea is not to get hit in the first place.

TRUTH: Neither is better. It depends on the specific application and your targeting.

MYTH: For combat, fixed blades are better than folding blades.

REALITY: Fixed blades are generally sturdier, longer and more adaptable to combative situations, while folding blades offer ease of carry, concealment and some legal advantages. For all out war, fixed blades are superior. The problem lies not with their tactical effectiveness, but with their legal justification. There is a distinct legal risk when carrying a fixed blade for the sole purpose of self defense.

TRUTH: Legal considerations aside, a knife is a knife is a knife. Effectiveness depends on the user.

MYTH: The ice pick grip is better than saber or hatchet grips.

REALITY: When you are facing someone who also has an edged weapon, I don't advise the use of the ice pick grip unless you're very close and very skilled. If you have the luxury of time and distance, the saber grip is much more useful because it offers the greatest reach and dexterity possible. The ice pick and other grips are tactical grips that are used in specific situations and for specific reasons.

TRUTH: The ice pick grip is effective as a close range trapping and finishing technique, while the saber grip is more versatile. Both are effective under the right circumstances.

MYTH: Today there are a lot of masters of knife fighting out there.

REALITY: No, but there are a lot of people claiming to be blademasters today. Claiming and being are two different things. Renewed interest in the blade as a defensive tool has sported a new growth industry. Whenever this happens and money is to be made, people seem to come out of the woodwork to capitalize on it.

TRUTH: There are very few legitimate masters of the blade.

MYTH: People who study martial arts and weapons craft are violent.

REALITY: For the most part, the opposite is true. Most people who actively study martial arts are good nonviolent people. As a matter of fact, the more someone studies, the less violent he becomes. You can often gauge someone's skill by his decline in ill temper. This is because almost any degree of mastery of the martial arts requires discipline and self control. Those people who cannot control themselves will not be able to reach any serious level of skill. Martial arts and weapons craft are not about violence. They are about self reliance and self control. The study and practice of them breeds self confidence that leads to restraint and nonviolent behavior patterns.

TRUTH: People who really study the arts of war are almost without exception nonviolent individuals. The achievement of real skill requires considerable discipline and self control, two traits which eradicate violent behavior.

CHAPTER FIVE

THE CUTTING EDGE

"Any weapon will do if you will do."

– Dr. Ignatius Piazza

An edged weapon is loosely defined as any blade, instrument or tool capable of cutting or puncturing the human body. That's a pretty broad definition. Under that umbrella, edged weapons include screw drivers, pens, pencils, glass and bottles, credit cards, keys or even a tooth pick. Certainly in a pinch you could use any of these, but for our purposes we are interested in knives designed specifically for self-defense.

When I was a kid, knives were either pocket knives or hunting knives. They came in various shapes and sizes showing little imagination or variation. They had no clips, quick opening mechanisms or special blades. A pocket knife was carried inside the pocket with your change. They were usually small, oblong in shape and sported at least several blades and other gadgets. You opened them by small groves in the top of each blade and they remained in place by the tension. A fixed blade or hunting knife was carried in a sheath.

A MODERN RENAISSANCE

Today things are different. About ten years ago there was a renaissance in edged weapons technology. It came on the wings of the custom knife makers and took flight

first in the firearms industry, when people became interested in alternatives to the use of the gun as a self-defense tool.

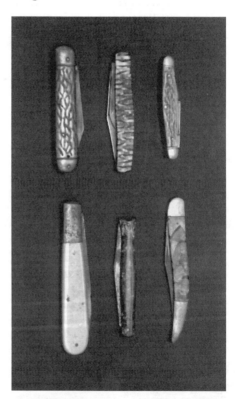

A few of my grandfather's pocket knives from the 1940's.

FOLDING VS. FIXED

Most knives fall into two distinct categories: fixed or folding blades. Most people are familiar with these two types. Fixed blades are knives with non-movable parts. Folding blades fold up into the handle for safety, ease of carry and concealment. The blades themselves also fall into two general categories with variations ad infinitum. Blades are either symmetrical, such as in double edged daggers, or asymmetrical like a bowie knife.

With this renaissance came new ideas, new methods, new metals and composites in a cornucopia of shapes and sizes. Companies like Spyderco and Benchmade grew into giants with the mass production of modern folding knives. We could write an entire book on the numerous types, styles and configurations of today's tactical folders, but this book is about knife fighting, not knife styles. If you want to know the details about different types of knives or knife making, there are quite a few publications on the newsstands or in your library; check them out. However, you need to be selective in your analysis of the information they provide. Remember that the vast majority of the people that write for and contribute to knife periodicals are writers, not fighters. Most (if not all) have never really sparred full contact (with knives or fists), and fewer still have ever been in a real fight in their lives. This lack of real experience can lead to some wild and outrageous techniques and tactics that could get you killed. For the most part, the majority of the information in these magazines is good because very little of it deals with knife combat itself. Like gun magazines, most articles deal with the new models, materials and gadgets available to the consumer. They are product-based. This is rarely a problem as long as you can separate the gadgets from the viable weapons.

Both types can be used to slash or thrust. Daggers have the advantage of the double edge and their stiletto-like point. Many daggers were originally designed to penetrate light armor and were long and slender. Asymmetrical weapons have the edge on one side. Both designs and their infinite variations are equally effective in trained hands.

CHOOSING A BLADE

Many fixed blades have the advantage of pure strength and combat-friendly design. Like miniature swords, they provide a handle, sometimes a pommel for striking and usually a guard which acts like a bracing mechanism for the hand so it doesn't slide up the blade when thrusting. Fixed blades are usually longer than folding weapons, which can definitely be an advantage in a real fight.

However, unless you can somehow justify carrying a fixed blade as part of your work or day-to-day life, you've got one major problem. If you use it, you may get yourself in trouble with the law. Let's say you're at the mall one day and you come across a knife shop. After browsing for a while, you find a beautiful combat fighting knife. It's nine inches long, ATS-34 steel with a serrated edge, black T (Teflon) finish, rubberized grips, checkered hilt and has a brass striking pommel. It even has a little logo on it, a skull and crossbones and the words "death dealer" etched into the steel. It's one scary knife. It is the perfect weapon to take to a knife fight, right? Wrong. Tactically, it sounds like a great weapon, and if I were going to war tomorrow, I'd like one just like it to go with my AR-15, .45 and fragmentation grenades. For war the double edged straight blade design is excellent. A thin straight blade permits thrusting motions between the ribs, into the throat or small targets like the eye. The double edge permits you to slash in any direction with equal effect. And a longer blade is also desirable. A three inch blade is useful for slashing, but for lethal thrusting attacks to the heart, lungs, groin or kidneys, longer blades are necessary to reach the vital organs, especially if the attacker has a large layer of fat, clothing or muscle to penetrate. It may make perfect sense to you to carry such a weapon for self protection, but not to most people.

But, unfortunately, this blade is your worst nightmare. Not because it won't be effective but because it will. Remember that we live in a society of rules and you will be judged by society's standards, not your own. If you carry a designated "fighting knife," you're already one step behind the game because it shows premeditation. If you use this weapon and find yourself in court defending your actions (from your attackers or his suing family), you will have to justify exactly why you were carrying it. It's a green light for prosecution, a prosecutor's dream. He can hold your "death dealer" up as evidence of violent forethought. You may want to own this weapon but don't carry it for self-defense. If

you do, you could find yourself living with the very people you defended yourself against, his friends or cousins and/or paying his family restitution for the rest of your life.

I myself have a vast collection of modern and antique swords, guns and knives of every type, but I wouldn't carry most of them for self-defense if you paid me. I do feel sorry for the burglar who breaks into my home though. For self-defense, I recommend nondescript, custom or production model folding blades. As a matter of fact, the more common the blade, the easier it will be to justify its use in a crisis. After all, everyone is carrying one these days.

HANDLES AND GRIPS

It used to be that folding knives were somewhat awkward to hold on to when defending yourself, because their handles weren't made for fighting. They were made to cover the blade. In combat, the handle and grip must serve multiple functions. The grip

must be such that if my hand becomes sweaty or covered with body fluids (a likelihood), the knife won't slip from my grasp. A checkered handle can be effective, as well as handles made of certain materials that have a porous or natural friction to them. Personally, I like rubberized grips like the ones found in some of the SOG and Cold Steel weapons. The user's ability to grip and retain the knife in battle is paramount. Therefore, the knife must have some type of thumb or forefinger bracing mechanism. This is because when thrusting the knife into the body you may encounter a wide variety of resistance to even the sharpest point. Penetrating soft tissue will not usually be a problem. However, if in the same thrust the tip of your weapon hits bone, it will likely come to an abrupt halt. Your hand will not. I'm sure you can see the problem. As a matter of fact, this is one of the most common injuries when a person uses a knife that isn't designed as a defensive tool. Without proper instruction, and a considerable modification of technique, the common kitchen knife could end up cutting your hand to ribbons. When selecting an edged weapon for self-defense, the first requirement is that you can hold onto it during a violent struggle. Whatever blade you choose, you should be comfortable that the grip and bracing features will provide a solid base and reduce the chance of slipping with hard contact.

QUALITY

Today almost anyone can go to his local mall, outlet store or swap meet and purchase an edged weapon. As a matter of fact, there are more edged weapons in every household, street, block and city in the world than any other weapon. Right now I'd be willing to bet that your kitchen has more knives in it than you have guns, and the same for your neighbor. However useful in a pinch, kitchen knives, screw drivers and scissors are not ideal fighting tools. You need a weapon designed to be a weapon but still unobtrusive enough to carry without reservation. Shop around and buy the best knife you can. Don't

buy junk. You wouldn't buy a cheap or poorly made gun so why would you buy a cheap tactical folder? If you might have to bet your life on a tool someday, purchase the best tool you can afford.

OPENING MECHANISMS

Syderco owns the patent on that little hole on the knife blade that you can hook your thumb in to flick it open. Various other buttons, indentions, plugs and screws now adorn modern tactical folders along with

automatic or "switchblade type" knives. Should you have a switchblade type knife for self-defense? Will you need to draw and open it instantly in a fight? Probably not. Certainly you should have a quick opening knife. You want to get it out and ready for action as quickly as possible, but the likelihood that your life will depend on deploying the blade in a split second is not very good. If you are in a predicament that requires that type of lightning reactions, you're better off leaving the blade where it is and reacting with whatever is at hand.

Today tactical folders are often so well made that having a switchblade type opening mechanism is really unnecessary. I prefer "kinetically open knives" or knives which can be opened by gravity or with a flick of the wrist. They are just as fast as the fastest switchblade and often come with better internal structures which make them sturdier than some mechanically opened blades. But the choice of a knife is yours. Just be sure to buy quality.

LOCKING MECHANISMS

Since the folding blade is in two parts, a strong locking mechanism is essential. Although there are a lot of clever blade locks, they come in two basic varieties, back locks and liner locks. In the back lock mechanism, a locking bar is built into the back side of the handle. When you press a small indention or grove, it separates the bar from the blade and allows it to be opened or closed. With a well built knife, there is usually no problem with this. However, when the knife is designed by a knife maker, not a knife fighter, the maker will sometimes place the release button at the crest of the handle which, under the pressure of certain combat grips, may cause an accidental release of the blade. Imagine slashing away at some thug and the next thing you know a few of your fingers are lying on the pavement.

The other common locking mechanism is a liner lock. It's called a liner lock because it is comprised of a bar which is offset to one side of the blade when closed. This bar is under tension and when the blade is opened, the bar snaps in place, coming in line with the blade itself. If well made, this is the closest thing to having a fixed blade. Strong and sturdy, the liner lock and variations thereof are a good bet for a combat folder. But even liner locks can fail. A student of mine once brought in a high dollar knife made by a famous knife maker (I'll mention no names). It was well made and sharp as a razor. On further inspection I saw that the liner lock looked a little funny, so I put some tension on it and snap! It folded in my grasp. Had I not reacted quickly and pulled may hands

away, I would have been severely cut. A knife is still just a man-made tool. It should be sharp. You should be able to open it and keep it open, and you should be able to hold onto it in a conflict. Beyond that, little else matters. Don't get lost in the details.

SERRATIONS

Serrations are the little sharklike teeth cut into some blades. Like a saw, they can help to cut through objects by focusing the friction of multiple edges on a single surface. Remember the Ginsu knives that burst forth on the market a decade or so ago? They were shown cutting through various things like tin cans, rope, and even steel cable, and then shown slicing a tomato with ease. Well it's not that the Ginsu knife was anything special. As a matter of fact, it was made of relatively cheap low carbon steel. The secret was in the serrations on the blade. They allowed the blade to retain its cutting ability and literally saw through objects that a normal straight blade would never penetrate. On a tactical folder or fighting knife, serrations can look rather evil, but are they necessary? Once again, if your knife is well made, serrations will matter very little. Cuts to the human body using a straight versus a serrated blade will look almost identical. A forensic pathologist will be able to decipher the difference, but the average person will not.

However, there is only one situation in which serrations offer a superior tactical advantage, and that is in the area of protective clothing. Even a razor sharp straight blade may not penetrate a thick denim or leather jacket if hit at certain angles. Serrations, however, act like miniature fangs that catch the fibers or grain of most materials and rip right through it. This being the case, I prefer serrated blades at least the first third closest to the hilt where you make contact with a slash.

OTHER TYPES OF BLADES

When it comes to weapons of war, man is exceedingly creative. There are an incredible number of variations on the edged weapon theme ranging from boot knives to push daggers, and from belt knives to small swords. All can be lethal in the right hands. All can be used to defend your life or take another. Beyond this, the most important thing to remember is that in self-defense you must justify your actions. If I were attacked in my study, it might be appropriate for me to draw my 16th century claymore from the wall and cleave my attacker in two. I might be able to justify it as an expedient weapon drawn from my environment in a time of need. On the street, push daggers and other assorted weapons of mayhem may be tactically effective, but legally lethal. Think before you act.

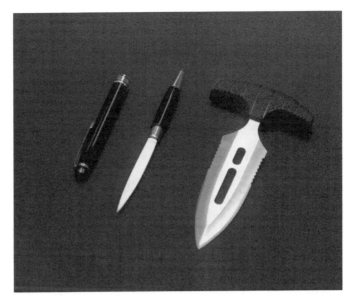

Edged weapons come in an incredible variety of shapes, styles and configurations. Some are designed to avoid detection while others are designed for maximum effect. However, if you choose to carry anything other than a basic folding knife, be prepared to do some explaining if you ever have to use it in self-defense. Carrying obviously lethal instruments can show premeditation and you could find yourself in trouble with the law. Simple is better.

CHAPTER SIX

THE SCIENCE OF THE BLADE

"Fighting is the applied science of force, motion and energy."
– Richard Ryan

With the renewed interest in knives and knife combat, numerous styles and theories have emerged on the horizon. Suddenly it seems there are a plethora of instructors teaching the art of the blade. Their systems range from the plausible to the inane. Some knife fighting styles are based solely on theory. They teach concepts and techniques that have little chance of working in the real world. After all, who is going to call them on it? Are you going to step up and challenge your knife fighting instructor to a real battle of steel to test his theories? Many knife fighting schools around today lack the critical element of reality. In training, reality is a must. There is no room for untested theories and techniques. What you learn must work, right now, the first time off the blocks. Because if you ever find yourself face to face with another highly motivated human being with a knife, you probably won't get to revise your tactics if they fail. Actually, if you are unlucky enough to come across a real knife fighter, it won't matter much because unless you're well trained yourself, you'll be dead before you know it. If you bet your life on steel, your techniques and tactics must be firmly rooted in reality. Leave the fantasy fighting to the movies.

Real combat can be sudden or drawn out. It can be initiated with explosive violent action or surgical precision. An attacker may jump you, taking you by surprise, or he may take a more wary tactical approach, feeling you out for your weaknesses before coming in for the kill. Either way, you must be prepared to survive a sudden attack as well as a variety of situations. To do this there are certain fundamentals that must be learned, the first of which is learning to adopt and maintain positions of advantage. These positions must allow you to deal with both the expected and unexpected. Neglect these fundamentals and you can be defeated easily, regardless of training or physical prowess.

POSITIONAL SCIENCE

In the science of the blade, positioning is everything. How and where you stand will determine to a great extent how effective you are, as well as tell your attacker a good deal about your skill, or lack of it. With proper combative positioning, a fighter can move with catlike quickness. He can attack with blinding speed and defend with fluid grace. Good positioning makes it infinitely harder to be struck with a decisive attack and immensely easier to execute one yourself.

Conversely, the fighter with poor body mechanics will be awkward, and seem to struggle for every move and action. He will be open to attack and counter and constantly seem to be behind the game.

The first step in learning to fight for real (with or without a weapon) is learning how to adopt positions of advantage at the outset of the conflict. Such positions will accentuate defensive ability while allowing access to offensive skills. In short, the first thing you must do is "out position" your attacker. Like a deadly game of chess, you position yourself so you can pounce on your prey and destroy him at the first opportunity.

POSITIONS OF ADVANTAGE

Effective body mechanics for combat start with proper balance and footwork. For our purposes, balance is defined as the ability to stay in a state of functional equilibrium and footwork is the ability to move quickly and easily during a conflict. Effective balance requires that you be both stable and mobile, and be able to move in virtually any direction at will. This requires that you adopt a neutral stance. Extremes in body positions usually cause problems. Widen your feet and lower your center of gravity as much as you can and you become very stable, but you sacrifice a degree of mobility. Bring your feet closer together and raise your center of gravity and you increase your mobility but sacrifice some stability. A neutral position is somewhere in between. It's called "neutral" because it is a position with enough stability to resist and generate force, and enough mobility to attack and evade at will. Neutral positioning allows fluid movement and sudden power in any direction when needed. This is the ideal platform to build your fighting skills upon, regardless of your size or physical abilities. To build this neutral fighting platform, let's start by covering a few principles that you need to know and show you how they relate

to your ability to fight effectively.

BASE OF SUPPORT

The base of support is the sum total of the distance between both your feet at any given time, above which your weight is supported. It symbolizes your contact with the earth. Because we are bipeds, our base of support is constantly in a state of flux. Take a step or alter your position, and your base of support changes. Too wide a base diminishes mobility, while too short a base affects our ability to generate and resist force. However, your base is infinitely adjustable, and you should learn to alter it to your advantage. For example, say you are fighting on a slick or wet surface. It would be a good idea to widen your base of support and keep your footwork simple in order to decrease your chances of slipping. Let your attacker slip and slide around. On the other hand, if you're a little rabbit (with fangs) and your attacker is a rhino, it might be a good idea to make sure you don't get trampled. You could shorten your base and use rapid footwork to avoid contact with his superior power. Both of these maneuvers represent tactical extremes. For the most part, you should adopt a base that allows for both mobility and stability, avoiding any extremes in either area.

CENTER OF GRAVITY

The center of gravity is that point inside the mass of an object at which the force of gravity affects it equally. Gravity acts on our bodies by pulling us to the earth along a constant vertical plane. Put simply, the center of gravity is that point at which my weight is equally divided on a vertical plane. A lower center of gravity contributes to an object's balance and stability because more of its weight is closer to the earth. Objects with a higher center of gravity are easier to move for the opposite reason. Understanding these principles allows you to manipulate your

A wide base of support and low center of gravity increase your stability by placing more of your weight closer to the earth and providing the body with a larger platform from which to function. It is wise to adopt such positions when power and stability are essential to performance. For example, you may increase your stability in order to grapple with a heavier or stronger opponent, to generate maximum power or if the terrain in which you are fighting is slick and unstable.

A small base of support and a high center of gravity increase your mobility by raising the body weight and decreasing the depth of weight distribution between your legs. You might adopt this positional extreme if quick movement is essential. Such tactics are effective in avoiding contact with superior power or when evasion is desired. From this position, it only takes a slight shift of weight or a movement of either foot to start you in motion.

Conversely, the more stable karate stance requires a much greater shifting of weight forward or backwards to put the body in motion. Both stances represent extremes in position that should only be utilized when it is obviously advantageous to do so.

The Dynamic Combat neutral fighting stance is designed to allow for both power and mobility. By avoiding extremes in body position, you can adapt to whatever might happen in a given situation. Although sometimes it becomes necessary to dramatically increase your stability and mobility, it is wise to avoid doing so unless it can obviously give you a dramatic tactical advantage.

level of stability or mobility at any given time. If the objective was to stand your ground and fight, it would be a good idea to widen your base and lower your center, becoming stronger and more stable, much like what a wrestler does before he ties up with his opponent. If you need to move rapidly, you would do the opposite, shortening your base of support and raising your center of gravity so you can move more quickly. And to become "neutral," you would find the middle ground between the two.

THE DRIVE LEG

Human beings are not very stable creatures. The average cat or dog is much more stable than we are, simply because it has a low center and four legs. In fact, most land mammals are quadrupeds having four legs and traveling close to the ground. Man, on the other hand, is a biped who stands upright with a large amount of weight distributed over a relatively small area, his feet. When you must resist or deliver force as you do in

a fight, you must place yourself in positions that will not be brought down easily. The base of support and the center of gravity contribute to your balance, but the critical element is the ability to use our legs to resist and generate force through proper body positioning. The only thing we have to brace ourselves against is the earth, so our connection to it is crucial. The drive leg is the placement of one leg behind the other in relationship to your immediate opponent. Its exact position is vital. For example, if you just stand upright, your legs provide you with some degree of potential power. The legs are designed for power and mobility. However, if you stand square facing an opponent directly with your feet parallel to him, you can't use the potential power of the legs. If he attacks you or just pushes you suddenly, you will fly backwards dramatically or fall to the ground. If the next time you face him, you place one leg behind you as a brace aligning your feet more perpendicular to his position, you will have acquired a drive leg. This rear leg acts like a brace dug into the ground behind you, remaining ready to deploy the large muscles of the legs to strike, move or generate force. These three concepts, the base of support, the center of gravity and the drive leg, form the mechanical triad on which combat functional balance is based.

help you. He can knock you easily off balance, or overwhelm you with more attacks than you can possibly handle with one side of your body. Tracking an attacker "on centerline" will keep you in the best position to fight back effectively.

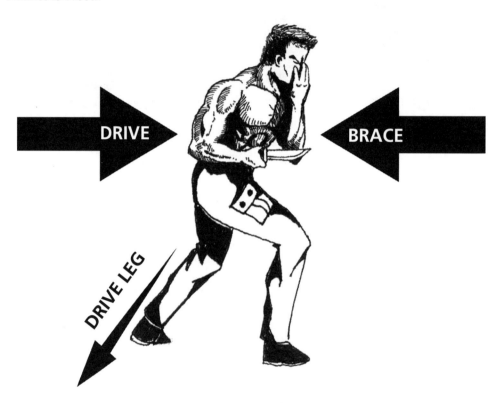

CENTERLINE

The final tactical positioning principle you need to know is the centerline. Centerline is an imaginary line that connects you and your immediate adversary. It's like a combative tracking device, a targeting line that keeps you in a position of advantage and maintains your drive leg during a fight. In combat, never let an attacker off centerline. This means that you should never let an opponent get an angle on your defensive position. If an attacker is able to get an angle on you, all your strength and positioning skills may not

KNIFE FIGHTING STANCES

The following stances (minus one of my design) are used by most knife fighting systems in the world today. They fall into a few distinct categories. Of course there are variations ad infinitum, but unless someone grows another limb somewhere, there will remain only so many positions you can adopt. Some are good fighting positions; some are not so good. Regardless, it needs to be said that any position you adopt that is successful is a good one. But as with everything in life, there is always good,

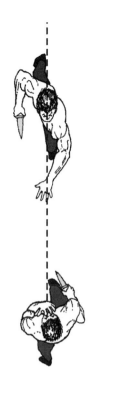

The centerline is an imaginary line that connects you to your immediate adversary. Its purpose is to help you maintain a position of advantage in a fight. Like the sights on a gun, it places your body and its weapons in the most favorable positions from which you may attack and counter attack.

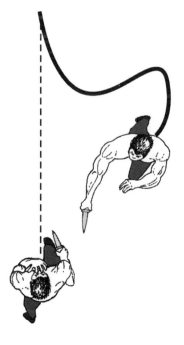

In combat, maintaining your centerline is critical. Lose you centerline and you can lose your life. An opponent who can get an angle off centerline can overwhelm you with more attacks than you can handle with a single limb defense. Loss of centerline also makes it much easier to disrupt your balance with very little force.

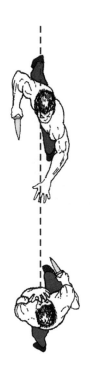

Footwork is the art of maintaining your position of advantage during a conflict. In most martial arts footwork is taught like dance steps. You're taught to step with one foot then the other in a specific way. Often, this is too complex and in a real encounter you won't be allowed to dance by the numbers. You'll have to adapt to what your opponent does.

In Dynamic Combat, complex movements are often simplified into concepts in order to make them easy to learn and apply. For example, the concept of footwork is to move in such a way as to maintain your balance and position at all times during the fight. In other words, the idea is to stay in your original stance position as much as possible, even in movement.

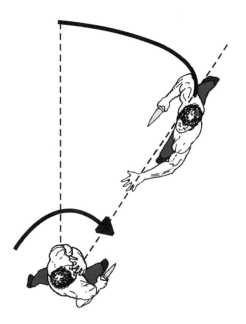

Centerline tracking is the ability to maintain your stable fighting platform as much as possible during the encounter. If an opponent moves or tries to get an angle on you, track him by turning to face him instantly. If you have to step, do so, but don't lean, shift your weight too much or cross your feet. Doing so disrupts your fighting position and can make you momentarily vulnerable to attack. Keep your footwork simple, taking short, quick steps to maintain your fighting stance.

better and best. In a knife fight, I'd put my money on the best. I will go over the strengths and weaknesses of the common stances and tell you why I believe mine is the best. Decide for yourself.

MILITARY STANCES

I'll start with military type stances because they are the most common. Traced back to the first world war, the military stance operates on sound defensive principles. Stand in a strong and stable position. Tuck the blade to your hip where your attacker can't get to it easily, and put one arm between you and him. Voilá, the military stance.

This position places the emphasis on defense and counter attack. The lead arm acts like a shield. A fighter will often sacrifice his front limb in order to get you with a decisive attack from the rear. This is neither good nor bad, especially if it works. There are times when it is good idea to adopt the shield forward positioning. For example, if you are cornered and cannot retreat, it might be wise to put up a good shield with the front arm, stand your ground and counter decisively. However, this position does limit the reach and access of the blade. In a knife fight, it is smart to put your claws in a position in which you can get to your attacker's body or limbs as fast as possible. The military stance does limit this ability to a considerable degree.

BOXER'S STANCE

Another common stance is the boxer's stance. Like a boxer, this position allows for quick, up-on-your-toes movement and a considerable degree of body evasion. Like boxing, there is a considerable degree of leeway in exactly how a person will stand in this position. Some will crouch down like a slugger and lash out quickly. Others will face more forward and stand more upright, preferring to be more mobile. Either variation can work.

Fighters in the boxer's stance often use the blade in the reverse or ice pick grip. It is amazing how many people advocate this position. Don't get me wrong, this position can be deadly, but it is not the best position to fight from in most conditions, especially against another knife fighter. The reverse position is a close range, trap and kill position. Unless you are lightning fast and your attacker has nowhere to go, I don't recommend it, especially for beginners. You must know exactly when, how and why to deploy it.

Nevertheless, this position is taught all the time. Often the knife fighter will move his hands in small, deceptive circles like a boxer and lash out suddenly. Whether crouched or upright, with the knife in the right or left hand, this stance offers a reasonable degree

of protection for the body targets (the hands are usually up in front of the chest) and a fast deceptive attack. Not bad, but considerably less effective when deploying any grip other than the ice pick.

HOLLYWOOD STANCES

It always amuses when Hollywood comes out with another action flick featuring a knife battle. Like the rest of the movie business, it's all sizzle and no steak. These choreographed battles look great, but don't

think for one minute that what you see on the big (or little) screen is real. Now there are some exceptions. A movie released a few years back starring Peter Coyote called *Exposure* was pretty good, especially the scene where Coyote witnesses a "persev" (short for perforate and sever) master knife fighter kill a couple of muggers in an alley in some third world country. They attack him and he dispatches them with such speed and ease that it approaches reality. But for the most part, what we see in the movies has little to do with the real world. In the movies, it's all big moves, flash and exaggeration. In real life, it's compact, sudden and deadly. A skilled knife fighter can strike in less than a

tenth of a second. A master can reach out and sever your jugular before you can blink. Once injured, he will swarm you with a deadly flash of steel, cutting your limbs and body to ribbons. End of story.

In the movies, heroes get shot, stabbed and beaten and still fight on to victory. In real life, take a bullet or a serious punch to the head and you go down. One serious cut to a limb and it can be immobilized. Cut an artery and you're dead. So what we see on the screen is for the most part profoundly unrealistic. Stances and techniques are employed for dramatic effect and suspense, not realism. Flailing the knife in the air threatening an attacker as in the movie *West Side Story* will only invite painful defeat by all but the most incompetent attacker. The good news is that most of what people know about knife fighting they got from watching movies and television. This is great! This is what you want. I would much rather face someone who learned his technique from Stephen Seagal movies than from one of my own students, or someone who has read my books and studied my videos.

TRANSITORY STANCES

Another form of combative positioning is the stance of no stance. I call these stance positions transitory because they are used by the knife fighter who operates from a variety of ever changing positions. The advantage is confusion. Like a magician, this type of stylist uses deception and slight of hand to keep his opponent guessing. If you're good, it can be quite deadly. While you try to figure out where the attack is coming from, whack! You're hit. If you have good footwork, balance and coordination, this tactic might work for you. But use it with caution. I learned a long time ago that if you stay calm against this type of fighter and simply plant a direct explosive attack down the middle, you can usually catch him.

THE DYNAMIC COMBAT
KNIFE FIGHTING STANCE

When my first edged weapons video came out under the Gunsite label, I was amused by one magazine reviewer who likened my stance to a "modification of the old military stance." This showed his ignorance and lack of practical experience. He was a writer not a fighter, and the subtle realities of my positioning concepts and their dramatic effect on real fighting eluded him. My stance is likened to a military stance in the same way a '64 Chevy is exactly like a Ferrari.

A stance is a position of advantage. It's like playing chess. The idea is to out position your adversary. When you play good chess there comes a point where one player's positions are superior to the other's, and the latter player is simply going to lose.

The DCM knife fighting stance starts with an awareness of centerline. We orient our position so that the opponent is directly in front of us. This is because it allows us to retain a position of advantage throughout the conflict. Imagine the centerline as an actual line connecting your body to his. Your feet are on either side of the line, one foot in front of the other, facing him directly. Find a neutral base of support and lower your center of gravity slightly by bending at the knees. Make sure your drive leg is in place.

In most situations you'll want to place your knife in the hand closest to your opponent, in front where you can use it. If you're right-handed, place the blade in the right hand and position the right foot forward. Reverse this position if you are left-handed. Although you can function from both positions (blade and foot back as opposed to forward), having the blade in front has enormous advantages. I know some instructors will have a fit about this. In fact, most knife fighting systems advocate blade back positioning. To explain why we do not, let's go back to the sword and shield analogy. If you were to have a sword in one hand and a shield in the other, you could stand with either side forward and still be effective. However, under most conditions, one position would be more effective than the other. To explain, let's imagine that you are a Roman gladiator thrown into the Coliseum to fight to the death for the amusement of the crowd. There is more than ample space to move about during the fight.

The Dynamic Combat knife fighting stance is the single most efficient platform from which to attack and defend with the blade.

In your right hand you hold the Gladius, a Roman short sword, and in the left a small forearm shield. Now you have a tactical decision to make. Whichever foot or side of the body you place forward toward the opponent will have the advantage of proximity. It will have quicker access. Do you place the sword in front or the shield? If you place the sword side forward, you will have greater access to the use of the blade. Therefore, the emphasis will be on offense with the shield providing supplementary defensive action. If you place the shield forward, it will provide a strong barrier between you and his sword. Your emphasis will then fall on defense and counter because the blade will take longer to get into play. The shield forward position would be good

if you are not in open ground where your movement is restricted. Under such conditions, your ability to stop an attacker's assault is essential. If you're not going anywhere, defense is critical.

When you can move, even a little bit, evasion becomes the primary form of defense, and offense and counterattack become your main focus. Movement takes the place of the need for a shield. Therefore it is safe to say that DCM has two versions of the same stance. One emphasizes defense and counter used in confined spaces, while the other emphasizes offense used whenever you can move. But the basics of positioning are the same. However, we only adopt blade back positioning when it is tactically advantageous to do so.

DCM STANCE POSITIONING

Keep your feet at a comfortable distance apart. Be sure to keep your feet and body facing somewhat forward. Wherever your feet go your body follows, so if you turn your back foot at 90 degrees, your body will begin to turn that way. It is much harder to attack and defend when your body is planed away from your attacker. You can't shy away from the fight. You must face the threat directly and deal with it.

DCM GUARD POSITIONING

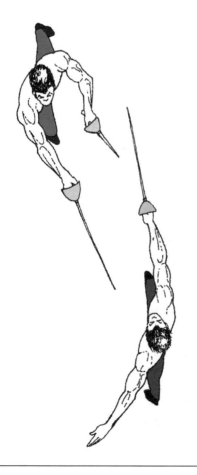

In and around the center of the body are our most vital organs, eyes, throat, heart and groin. These are the primary areas we want to both attack and defend. A severe wound in these locations could be very serious. Areas in which you might be able to take a knife attack are the extremities, the large muscle groups of the arms, legs, shoulders and back. As a general rule, the outside extremities are not as important as the central line of the body where penetrating attacks could mean death. You must cover and

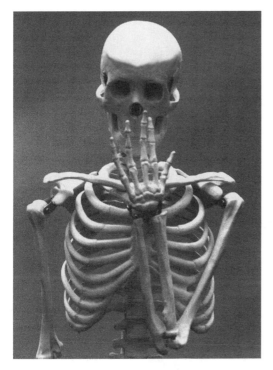

superior blocking skills and that's hard to do when someone swarms you with a blade. To survive, realize that you must have a last ditch line of defense in case something breaks through your outer guard.

To provide the best protection, the rear arm is brought forward in front of the body, placed vertical on your centerline. This does several important things. It brings your elbow out in front of the body, covering at least part of the abdomen from attack. Secondly, it forms a "cross beam bone structure" placing a column of vertical bone and muscle in front of the body. This, coupled with the already existing horizontal bone structure of the ribs, provides a strong cage for the vital organs we must protect. Also, it puts a hand right in front of your neck. Keeping this hand in this position covers the soft tissues of the throat, shielding them with the bones of your hand and wrist. In a worst case scenario, say a person gets through your other defenses, keeping this hand in position provides you with a last ditch shield against having your throat cut. It also helps you to keep your shielding hand out of harm's way. In many other stances in

protect these areas at all times. The ability to protect the central line from attack was critical in my development of a functional knife fighting position. Without such protection, a fighter would have to rely on

By placing the guard hand in front of the body and crouching, you can dramatically increase your defensive position. The humerus, ulna and radius bones of the arm help protect the thorax and vital organs. Crouching compresses the ribs and diminishes target surface pulling the lower abdomen out of immediate reach, thereby allowing you to focus your defensive concentration in the upper body.

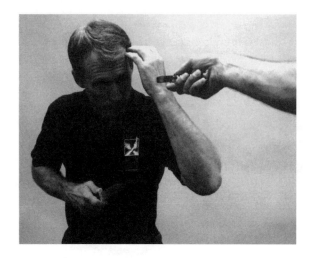

Keeping your arm in position throughout the fight provides you with one final barrier that an attacker must penetrate before reaching your vital targets.

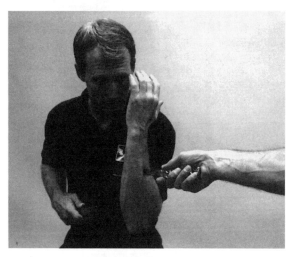

Even in a worst case scenario you may take a cut to the arm. Such a cut is unlikely to immobilize you, allowing you to fight on, at least temporarily.

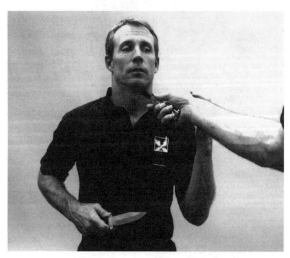

If you adopt an exposed stance, or you drop your guard in action, you could be killed in one fatal strike. Keep your guard up at all times.

Whether your right or left leg is forward, the upper torso remains in the same protected position. The blade is at your side and pointed at the adversary.

which the hand is "out there somewhere," people often find that when the heat is on and they're fighting fast and furious, they cut themselves as their defensive hand inadvertently strays into the fray. By keeping it tight and close to the body, you know where it is at all times.

THE BLADE HAND

There are all sorts of positions in which you can place the knife in a fight. Some people try to stick the knife in your face, using it as an instrument of intimidation. Others keep the knife hand far away from an opponent, trying to shield it from attack. If you stick something out there, it is going to get cut off. If you shield your weapon too much, you can't use it when you need it. Neither of these concepts works. You must position the blade where you can both protect it and use it at will. This is a simple matter. With your arm hanging relaxed to your side, simply raise the arm until the forearm is horizontal and pointing at your opponent. If you do this naturally, the mid point of the forearm should be directly at your hip. If your hand is at your side, the weapon is too far away. If your elbow is at your hip, the weapon is probably too exposed.

PUTTING IT ALL TOGETHER

To adopt the Dynamic Combat knife fighting stance, first grip the weapon in the saber grip and place your right foot forward. Reverse the procedure if you are left-handed. The rear shielding hand comes up and protects the central line of the body. The forearm is vertical and bones of the hand and wrist cup the chin for protection. The blade hand tucks in to the side, with the blade pointing at the opponent at all times.

THE COMBAT CROUCH

Okay, now you have the basics of my stance. It offers the best platform for the use of the blade. But you're still vulnerable if you stand too upright. Standing with the back straight in an upright or rigid position elongates the body, exposing more surface area to attack. Standing tall means that you have to protect your entire body. Attacks could go to the head and neck, the area between the chest and groin or the legs themselves. This requires too many decisions with too much area to protect. In a knife fight, you don't want to get it wrong one out of three times. You don't have that type of margin for error.

By comparing the Dynamic Combat knife fighting stance to others, you can clearly see its advantages.

The military stance provides a strong fighting platform, but it has some distinct tactical disadvantages. The blade is too far back, making it slower and more telegraphic to use. This position also limits reach, especially to the opposite side of the body.

Boxer and similar stances provide a little better protection by keeping the hands up, or at least somewhere in front of the body. Unfortunately, the central line is still very much exposed to attack. The body is upright and vulnerable.

By comparison, you can see that the Dynamic Combat knife fighting stance is far superior to all other positions. A shield of bone covers the central line of the body. The crouch position not only makes for a much smaller target surface, but pulls the lower abdomen out of reach of the attacker. The blade is tucked in tight and becomes almost invisible.

Avoid these common mistakes. In this position, the defender is leaning too far forward exposing the head and throat to attack. His body is turned too far sideways and tilted off balance. Also, the blade is back and pointed toward the ground and the defensive hand is too low.

This position is better. It is more balanced and neutral with the blade forward. However, the defensive hand is high but too extended. An attacker can reach around it and get to the vitals easily. The base of support is also too wide with the rear leg in a locked position that doesn't allow for any thrust or movement.

This stance is correct. The body is balanced and neutral, having an equal degree of both mobility and stability. The weight is evenly distributed between both feet allowing for movement in any direction without adjustment. The defensive hand covers the central line of the body, protecting the throat, heart and abdomen. The blade hand is in a protected but effective position allowing for instant access to offense and defense.

When you crouch, you compress the body making it smaller and more compact. In a knife fight, smaller is better. This, coupled with your DCM guard positioning, makes it immeasurably harder to get through to a vital area. But the act of crouching has even more subtle advantages. When you crouch, the body forms an "S" shape. By bending at the waist, your torso is further back than your face. This provides a tremendous advantage because suddenly an attacker has to travel a much greater distance, through your blade and guard, to get to the heart, abdomen and legs. The combat crouch helps to pull the lower torso out of the fight and protect it. This limits the opponent's accessible target surface and makes your defensive decisions much easier.

GRADIENT POSITIONING CONCEPT

There you have it. It is the single best knife fighting stance in the world. When adopted, you automatically have a tremendous edge (no pun intended) against every other knife fighting stance out there. From this position, you can attack and defend with equal ease.

It is designed to give you the advantage when fighting another individual who is also skilled with the blade and will work even better against the uninitiated.

However, this position is gradient, meaning that you don't always have to adopt it in its extreme. You don't have to always crouch as low as you can or hold your hands strictly in position. If you are able to keep your distance from an opponent, you can relax more. The distance allows you more reaction time to snap back into the stance when you need it. Also, a more upright and less compact position is more mobile and you may need that under some circumstances. But if your movement is restricted, or you face an extreme threat, assume the position as intended and stay there. It just may save your life. Perhaps the hardest thing is maintaining the stance when in movement. To be effective, you must practice keeping in your stance when you move, attack, or defend as much as possible. Leaving this position, even momentarily, means exposure and possible counterattack, so strive to make staying in your stance second nature.

CHAPTER SEVEN

THE ART OF THE CUT

"Invincibility lies in defense, the possibility of victory in the method of attack."

— Sun Tzu

The edged weapon provided man with what mother nature did not, sharp claws. The knife is man's version of the claw or talon. In nature, claws are used to spear, rip and tear a prey until it is rendered defenseless. So it is with the blade. Fundamentally, the object of the use of an edged weapon for survival is to puncture vital body targets or to slash the vulnerable body areas until the opponent ceases to function. In self-defense, this may mean a single slash on the arm or an overwhelming all-out assault to end an attacker's life. But for either to be effective, you've got to be able to use the weapon with pinpoint accuracy. In the fifties, the famed firearms expert, Bill Jordan, was quoted as saying that, "Speed is fine, but accuracy is final." This is the essence of the effective use of the blade. In other words, it's great to be fast, but you've got to hit what you aim at. Although you can attack any part of the body with an edged weapon in a time of need, you should confine your targets to those body areas which are most likely to cause the most shock and trauma.

The human body is a strange amalgamation of strong and weak, soft and hard, vulnerable and invulnerable. Consider the fact that a slash just beneath the jaw to the throat can cut through skin and muscle, and if deep enough, sever a major artery and you could die in one swift stroke of the blade. The very same slash to the jaw itself will cut skin and mark bone, but leave you with only a scar to show for it. And the difference between the two outcomes could be only a fraction of an inch.

BLEEDERS

Targets fall into three distinct categories: bleeders, immobilizers and sudden death targets. Bleeders are targets designed to open up the cardiovascular system of the body. The arterial system moves the oxygenated blood from the heart to the vital organs and extremities, while the veins return this blood to the heart to be replenished. This happens countless times every day keeping the system functioning. Because arteries lead from the heart, they are under pressure. As such, they are thicker and stronger than the veins. Think of them like a garden hose capped off at the end. When you turn the water on, the hose becomes pressurized. What would happen if you took a pin and popped a hole in the hose? You would instantly get a violent spray of water. If you were to slash the hose, the water would surge forth at a rapid rate. So it is with arteries.

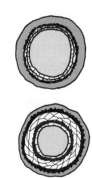

Arteries conduct blood away from the heart under high pressure and their structure reflects this. The walls of the arteries are thicker and more resilient than the veins.

Puncture one and the heart forces the blood out of the body rapidly.

Veins, on the other hand, are not under pressure. Puncture them and we still bleed but not as fast. In a life and death encounter, a master knife fighter will endeavor to attack the opponent's arterial system whenever possible because he knows that one good cut will end the battle quickly. How fast will it end with an arterial bleeder? Well, it depends on factors like pulse rate, location and type of cut and whether the cut remains checked or unchecked. But unless you get immediate medical attention, an arterial cut usually means death within minutes. But that's not the worst of it. The really bad news is that an arterial puncture will produce a rapid loss of blood pressure and, although you may be able to physically survive for a number of minutes, such a loss in pressure will mean unconsciousness in ten to sixty seconds. In other words, with a serious arterial wound, even if you could continue fighting you'll pass out in seconds from a rapid loss of blood pressure. This is why it's so imperative to use evasion and to fight from a stance that protects your vital targets from sudden attack.

In a life and death struggle with the blade, one of the primary objectives is to open up the pressurized blood vascular system of the body. Cutting, puncturing or stabbing the heart or major arteries will produce massive blood loss and a subsequent drop in blood pressure, which will induce unconsciousness and death within minutes if it does unchecked.

The heart can be accessed with direct power stabs which can puncture the sternum and cause death instantly. This is another reason why you don't want to expose the central line of the body. Access to the arteries is more difficult. The primary zone of access is in the throat. Deep cuts in this area can puncture or even sever the common carotid and subclavian arteries. One of the most common misconceptions about arterial attacks is that you can easily access them through the wrists and at other joints of the body. Although this is possible, it is not easy to do because they are protected by muscle and tendon.

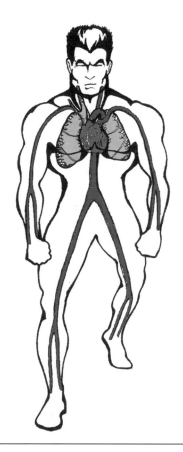

The best targets of access for the arterial system are the throat, deep into the center of the body near the spine, under the armpit, the upper and inner thigh for the femoral artery and, if cut deep enough, the wrists and the underside of the arms themselves.

IMMOBILIZERS

Immobilizers are targets that cut muscle, tendons, ligaments and connective tissue and destroy the function of the skeletal muscular system. I'll give you a brutal example. Say you're faced with a serious attacker who has extensive karate training. He attacks you relentlessly with vicious kicks to your stomach and groin. You evade his attacks, but he corners you and you access your knife. Undaunted, your attacker throws another front kick toward your groin, but instead of obliging him, you pivot slightly to the side and catch his leg with your guard hand and before he can react, you cut deeply with a lifting slash severing the tendons on the back of his knee. He is immobilized and may never walk the same again. Slashing immobilizers include attacks on or around any joint. Stabbing immobilizers create pain, shock and trauma by driving the blade into the belly of a muscle or directly into a joint itself. To be effective, such tactics must cut deep and accurately. In a way, they are more humane than taking his life with a bleeder attack, but they will still leave a permanent mark. Immobilizers could cripple an opponent for life.

SUDDEN DEATH TARGETS

Sudden death attacks are designed to end the situation with one decisive strike. They are strikes targeted to the most vulnerable

Immobilizers are targets designed to hinder, disrupt or destroy the function of the body. If your body is no longer works, it's hard to use it to fight with. Since the limbs are used to attack, defend and hold tools, they are the primary focus of the immobilization attack. For example, say you're in a situation where you must fight back, but it is not yet to the point where lethal force (such as an arterial attack) is called for. In such a situation, you might bury the blade to the hilt into the attacker's outer thigh and run. Doing so would probably discourage any pursuit on his part.

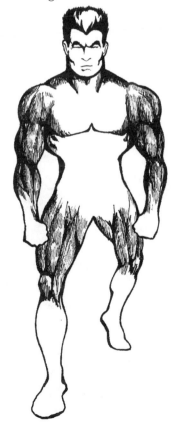

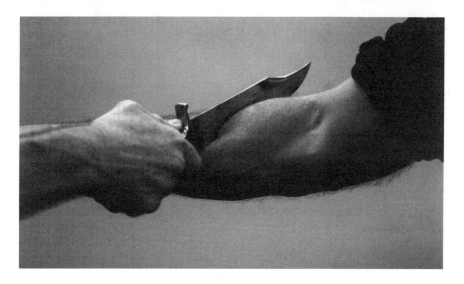

Immobilization attacks to the arms can be very effective as long as they are delivered accurately. Severing the muscles and tendons destroys the function of the hand and arm itself, often rendering it useless. Here the defender cuts through the brachioradialis muscle of the upper forearm, and the interosseous and related tendons of the lower arm which are responsible for the raising of the lower arm and grip strength.

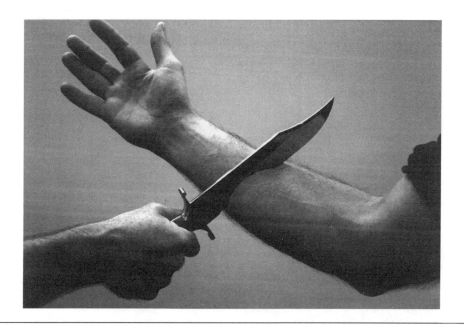

Here Ryan demonstrates the devastating effect that an immobilization attack can have on an attacker.

From the ready position, Lance throws a quick, powerful kick to the stomach. Ryan rides the kick out slightly and checks it with his guard hand.

Before he can withdraw his leg, Ryan loops the blade under the back of the knee and pulls the knife toward him, severing the posterior thigh muscle or the connective tissue on the back of the knee itself. A deep cut in this location would make it impossible to contract the lower leg.

Ryan throws the leg off centerline, exposing his flank to attack.

Before he can recover, Ryan moves in and traps his upper arm, holding him in position...

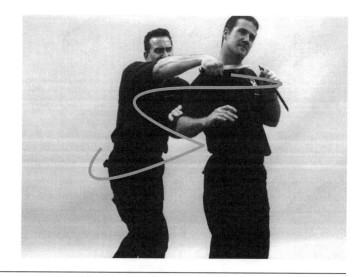

...stabs the lower abdomen and immediately flows into an attack to the throat.

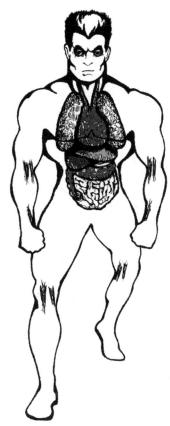

Sudden death targets are designed to produce immediate effect and end the conflict within the shortest possible time frame. The idea is to limit your assault to the most vital and vulnerable areas of the human body and to attack them with maximum speed and power. When your life is on the line and you only have a few precious seconds to take action, attack these areas with full speed and force until the attacker goes down or you find a way to escape the encounter.

EYES

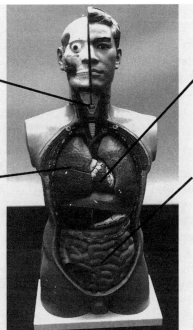

THROAT   **HEART**

LUNGS   **COLON**

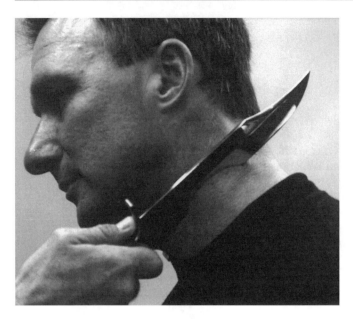

avoid a nasty situation. The attacker may decide that running is better than dying. Most scumbag criminals are not likely to engage someone who might best him in a fight to the finish. For this reason, an air of confidence, no matter how hard it is to muster, can go a long way to ending a confrontation without bloodshed. Don't misunderstand. I am by no means advocating that you try to use the knife to bluff your way out of a bad situation. If you draw your knife, you had better be prepared to use it in any way necessary to protect yourself. Let's explore the common knife fighting grips and discuss their advantages and liabilities.

body targets and are delivered with maximum speed and leverage. Examples are punctures to the heart, eyes, groin or even into the brain cavity itself. Such targets are for life and death situations only and require considerable accuracy and luck to hit, especially on a moving target. Therefore, unless the attacker gives you an obvious opening (and you're pretty sure he's not smart enough to be baiting you), don't go for these until you have slowed the attacker down. However, if your life depends on your next move, sudden death targets may be your only and best option.

GRIPPING THE BLADE

How you stand and grip the blade is of critical importance. A grip is a method of holding the blade in combat. Your positioning, the type of weapon and the grip you choose to use will dictate to a large extent what you can and cannot do with the blade. How you hold the knife and the positions you adopt are important in its use as well as the psychological impact it may have on an attacker. Even a novice, using the proper grip and giving the appearance of being an expert in its use, may

THE SABER GRIP

The saber grip got its name from the use of the saber and foil in fencing. With the blade diagonal across the palm and the thumb and forefinger behind the guard, the blade is pointed forward like an extension of the forearm. The saber grip is the most versatile

and effective grip for knife combat because it allows a great deal of control and manipulation. I call it the "surgical grip" because it allows for the most dexterous use of the blade at both long and close range. With this grip, you can thrust and slash in almost any direction with equal ease. Moreover, the saber grip provides an optimum striking radius representing the fullest extension of the arm and blade. The only real disadvantage is that the knife's side-to-side stability is not as good as some other grips. If you don't grip it tightly or strike with the wrong edge, it is possible that it could be dislodged. Make sure you are striking with the right edge all the time.

THE ICE PICK GRIP

The ice pick grip is used like a predator's talons. Like the claws of an eagle or tiger, the blade can be retracted or articulated at will. Gripping the blade tightly in the fist with the blade pointed down, the ice pick grip overcomes the stability problem of the saber position. Unlike the saber grip which relies primarily on finger pressure, the ice pick employs the strongest muscles of the entire hand for its stability. The knife is unlikely to

slip from your grasp in a fight. The grip also makes it easy to conceal a drawn knife behind the forearm, adding the possibility of the element of surprise to your attack. The drawback is that your reach is less than that of the saber. Also, with this grip high targets to the face and neck are easy to attack with stabs, but more difficult to reach with slashes because the position of the blade and your wrist allows for only limited movement.

THE HATCHET GRIP

The third common grip is called hatchet grip. Most novices instinctively hold the knife this way. It is the reverse of the ice pick position, and it is stronger than the saber because it uses the entire hand, just like the ice pick, but the blade protrudes upward toward the thumb, instead of downward away from it. Like the ice pick, your blade articulation is diminished by limited wrist movement. But this grip is strong and exceptionally good for power stabs, slashes or close-range flanking attacks.

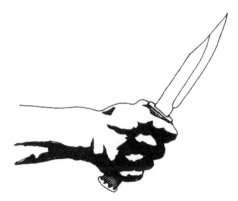

There are quite a few other grips, but they are mostly variations on the theme and a few are ridiculous and shouldn't be taken seriously. Grips other than the big three mentioned here are for advanced tactical combat and used only by someone who knows exactly how they can give him an advantage. I'll cover such techniques in my next book on this subject. That being said, here are two alternative grips you could consider.

REVERSE SABER GRIP

The reverse saber position is an exaggerated ice pick grip used almost exclusively for surprise attacks and at very close range. The knife runs parallel to the arm with the blade pointed toward the elbow. With the blade tilted back toward the forearm, it can remain hidden until needed. It's best not to use it with a double-edged blade for obvious reasons. Utilized only in specific situations, this grip is not a good long-range fighting grip. Its advantage is much like a backward talon seen on some ancient dinosaurs. Many raptors had one or more razor sharp claws that angled back toward their bodies and

limbs. They would explode at their prey, extending their talons as they pounced, knocking their prey to the ground and effectively eviscerating it. It you can get the jump on a attacker and are confined to very tight quarters, this type of grip is viable.

THE FOIL GRIP

This is a terrible grip for most serious combat situations. In this position, the blade and handle are placed in the hand flat (horizontal), and the blade is used to flick and poke at an adversary. The one advantage is that it can be used for quick, rapid-fire rips and dicing motions. Perhaps if you just wanted to intimidate someone who was threatening you, and didn't want to seriously hurt him, you may surprise him with a quick flicking attack from the foil grip. But for the most part, I don't recommend it. It can be useful with certain types of blades though. Thin blades with short handles and no guards work well with this grip. You can

wrap the fingers around it and brace the handle against the butt of the palm. This can be useful as a stabbing weapon because, in this position, it is likely that it will slip between the ribs and its horizontal position can be effective in cutting the arteries in the throat. Other than that, catalog it in your arsenal as trivia.

TYPES OF CUTS

When an animal attacks its prey, it doesn't think about exactly what type of cut it will use with its claws or teeth. Nor does it think about exact targeting. Animals attack and kill out of instinct. They use their teeth and claws without forethought and deliberation. They attack whatever they can reach with whatever they can. In application, this is how you must learn to fight - action by instinct. But the animals have one distinct advantage that humans don't have. Their teeth and claws are part of them. They are attached and integrated into their neural muscular system. This makes it infinitely easier to use them instinctively. Man, on the other hand, has to hold his weapons. He has to manipulate his claws in an exact manner to be effective. He has to learn how to cut.

SLASHES

A slash uses the edge of the blade as it is drawn against and across a target. When steel meets human flesh, flesh loses and a slash can open up large wounds. This is because the skin is somewhat elastic and, when severed, the tissue separates around the wound. For a slash, the point of contact on the blade should be low, close to the guard, to ensure a drawing motion across the surface to be cut. This point is also the strongest point at which the hand and the blade meet, which helps to maintain control of the weapon during an exchange.

STABS

Stabs are puncture wounds created by the penetration of the tip of the blade followed by its length into the body. On the surface, a puncture wound may appear as a small slit, but stab wounds are more likely to be life threatening because they let fluid out and air in. The potentially lethal effect comes from what the knife does as it enters the body cavity. It can puncture internal organs or sever vital systems causing massive trauma with a single stroke. Depending on the location, a single deep puncture could be almost instantly lethal.

THE TECHNIQUE OF CUTTING

In combat, cutting must be done with the utmost speed and control. You must learn to lash out in a fraction of a second, hit what you aim at, and recover before you can be countered. It sounds simple, but unless you have had extensive combat martial arts training or are a gifted athlete, it takes some practice to master. The ability to strike swiftly and accurately is the most important and fundamental skill with the blade. With this ability, it is possible to end an encounter almost before it has begun with a single decisive attack.

SPEED

Physiologically, some people are innately faster than others. Just as the potential for greater size or strength is genetically bred into some people, the ability to move quickly is to some extent a gift of nature. But everyone can learn to become faster than they are right now, and there are several ways to do it. The first way is simply by learning to relax the body's muscles while in action. Body tension acts like a break on the body's musculature system, slowing us down by making the muscles of the body work against each other. Your muscles are designed to work in opposing pairs. In any action, one set of muscles takes the role of the agonist, contracting to create a motion, while another set, the antagonists, must relax to allow this to happen. If you remain in a relaxed state, the muscle groups work together to create fast, fluid motion. When you tense up, you tighten both muscle groups and the agonist acts like a brake, fighting against the prime mover. So the first and foremost secret to speed is to keep the body loose and catlike during action. It helps to remember that the knife is a touch weapon and requires very little strength to be effective. Getting the blade to your target in a sudden explosive manner is far more important than the physical force behind it. You don't have to force your motions or "push" them with power. Stay loose. Stay relaxed and let the knife do most of the work.

Once you've learned to relax, you can further improve your speed by learning to economize your motions through directness. This advantage is best explained by analogy. Take two sprinters. Runner number one, Rick, is younger, stronger and faster than runner number two, John. They are standing at the starting blocks of a circular track. The object of the race is to get to the other side of the track, exactly opposite their starting point. John, being slower, has a distinct disadvantage. If he runs a conventional race he will probably lose. They set in the blocks, and "bang" the gun goes off. Rick flies off the blocks and around the track. But no matter how fast he, is he will never beat John, because at the gun, John took an abrupt left turn and ran across the field directly to the finish line. Sure, it's cheating in a conventional sense, but that's not the point. The end result was to get to the other side as quickly as possible and the shortest distance between two points is a straight line. John was physically slower, but more economical about reaching his goal. So it is with the blade. You don't need extreme distance or momentum. You need to get to your target directly. Learn to streamline your actions, stripping away all unnecessary motions you need to achieve your immediate objective. Just get the knife there and it will do the rest.

The last method for improving your speed is the old fashion way. Repetition. Yes, good old practice. By doing anything over and over again with intensity, the body adapts with time in an attempt to make it easier for us. The more you do, the more efficient you become. There is no substitute for intense training. Practice your key moves over and over again until they become second nature and your body will do the rest.

ACCURACY

Remember that "speed is fine, but accuracy is final." A lightning fast cut delivered to the mandible will cut the jaw and really anger an attacker. The same strike a half an inch lower could sever the carotid artery and kill in less than a minute. Same strike, same striker, different target. Accuracy, (essentially eye-hand coordination), is relatively easy to improve through repetition. The mind's sense of distance, your reach and kinetic sense are dramatically improved with practice. But you can't hit what isn't there. You need a target. If you have rubber training knives and protective gear, the best target is another person. If not, get something you can strike, such as a heavy bag, speed bag, a towel draped over something, a pillow or even the leaves on a tree. Find something to focus your attacks on. A simple but challenging accuracy device is a tennis ball on the end of a small piece of rope. With a black marker, print several numbers on its side: 1, 2, 3, etc. Stand just outside the kill zone and strike the ball with a stab or a slash of your practice blade, or you can place some duct tape on the edge of a real knife. The ball will whip and spin out of control with your strike and the number will blur, but stay

ready, because the moment you can read a number, strike out again! In this way it becomes a reactive accuracy drill. Keep the eyes open and clear. Look directly at your target and strike swiftly. Do this stationary and in motion to constantly challenge your sense of reach and distance. When you can hit the ball consistently and with great speed, you know you can hit a target on the opponent's body. For a real challenge, mount several balls in the same place and strike them alternately.

STRIKE EXTENSION

In a real knife fight the last thing you ever want to do is trade slashes and stabs. Standing toe-to-toe and slashing it out will most likely get both of you your own slab at the county morgue. Only a fool would think that he can move into the kill zone of another knife fighter and block and counter every single strike thrown at him. This is movie stuff. If you miss a block in a knife fight, you could be dead. You should always try to use the advantage of reach and distance. If possible, maintain as much distance from your opponent as you can as often as you can. When you strike, explode forward just enough to reach out and hit your target and recover instantly. Use your full reach. When practicing, extend your striking distance by taking a step with each attack and striking with full arm extension. You can always shorten it up if you have to. Remember that the edged weapon extends your reach by the length of the blade, but you can only use this to your advantage if you use maximum arm extension.

THE USP -
UNIVERSAL STRIKING PATTERN

The other primary combative attribute of the knife is that it is multidirectional. Like a clawed hand, it can strike at any target you could reach and from any angle or position you could get into. This is one of the factors that makes the blade such a great weapon and, second to the gun, the ultimate equalizer. You could deliver lethal counterattacks standing, in a head lock, bent over a car or table or on the ground. As long as you can get to your blade and some part of the attacker's anatomy, you can use it effectively. In order to practice this versatility factor, a striking pattern was developed. This pattern allows the practitioner the luxury of practicing a wide variety of attack angles at one time. This promotes a sense of flexibility and adaptability in attack and defense. However, this is not a strict pattern to be adhered to or to be used as examples of attack combinations. It is simply a catalog of movements designed to promote striking flexibility. The pattern is comprised of eight circular attacks, followed by two linear attacks and two semicircular attacks for a total of twelve steps in all. Once learned, it represents virtually all attack angles.

Ryan leads a large group class in the practice of the universal striking pattern. The USP provides the student with a catalog of movement designed to allow for easy practice of all angles of attack.

1. *Diagonal downward 10:00 to 4:00*
2. *Diagonal downward 2:00 to 8:00*
3. *Horizontal 9:00 to 3:00*
4. *Horizontal 3:00 to 9:00*
5. *Diagonal upward 8:00 to 2:00*
6. *Diagonal upward 4:00 to 10:00*
7. *Vertical 12:00 to 6:00*
8. *Vertical 6:00 to 12:00*
9. *Linear high to zero*
10. *Linear low to zero*
11. *Diagonal forward*
12. *Diagonal forward*

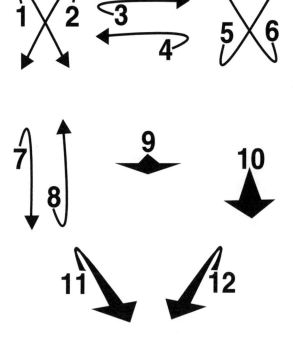

The universal striking pattern or USP is a catalog of the basic attack angles with the blade. When learned, it provides the student with a continuous fluid method of practice in the delivery of the most common strikes you will deploy.

ADVANCED CUTS

As you progress in ability, more advanced techniques of cutting methods become possible. A blademaster is able to use his weapon with deadly and surgical precision. With lethal grace he can surgically destroy an attacker in a ballet of blood and steel, and one of the tools he uses is the knowledge of advanced cutting methods. The following cutting techniques constitute the most effective and decisive use of the blade in a violent encounter. They are brutal and should only be used in an extreme life and death struggle. A warning here: No matter how fast you are, these cuts are more complex than simple stabs and slashes. They are vicious. They take more time and commitment to execute. Don't even consider their use unless you are legally and morally justified and, even then, they should only be used to finish a life and death struggle.

DICE CUTS

Dice cuts are rapid-fire short stroke slashes designed to inflict massive localized damage. They're usually used when someone has a hold of you, or to escape from a grappling situation using a knife. To execute, "slap and slide" the blade across the target as rapidly as possible, much like you would dice a stalk of celery. The result is a horrendous wound that slashes the flesh of a small area to ribbons. Although you could use the dice cutting concept anywhere, good targets are just about anywhere in the hand, arms or face. This technique is exceptionally good when applied as a release from a choke or other grappling holds.

FILLET CUTS

Fillet cuts are one of the most gruesome cuts with the blade because they are designed to tear the flesh from the limbs. Although they are rarely lethal, they can be psychologically

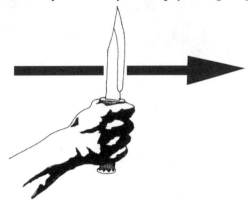

devastating. Fillet cuts are executed by running the edge of the blade parallel with the limb, cutting the flesh and muscle away from the bone. Done offensively, they are executed like a punch. Against an attack such as a punch, the blade can remain in place, intercepting the attack at a slight angle with the energy of the strike doing the damage.

GOUGE CUTS

A gouge cut creates a vicious puncture wound. Unlike dice cuts which slash the surface and muscle tissue, the purpose of a gouge is to inflict greater localized trauma inside the body. Instead of stabbing in and out of the body in a piston-like manner, a gouge cut rotates at the point of contact, opening the wound cavity dramatically.

Advanced cutting techniques can be brutally effective without necessarily being lethal. For example, here a fillet cut intercepts a punch and separates the skin from the attacker's arm. Below, a dice cut is used to shred the attacker's inner forearm and effect a release from a violent grab.

Gouge cuts are like exploding bullets. They enter the body and create massive internal damage. To execute, grip the knife as hard as you can. If you don't, the rotating action could remove it from your grasp. Deliver a linear stab, but don't extend the arm all the way. As the blade enters the body, violently rotate the elbow clockwise or counterclockwise.

RIP CUTS

A rip cut is perhaps the most vicious of all because it can cause the greatest trauma. Certainly it will create the largest wound cavity of any single stroke. One caution: The likelihood of anyone surviving a rip cut is slim to none. These cuts are highly likely to kill in one stroke and should be kept in the back of one's arsenal for use in the most extreme situations or emergencies.

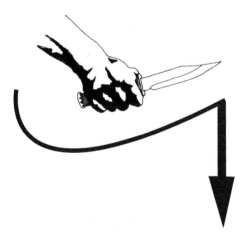

To do a rip cut effectively requires the use of leverage and the weight of the body. To execute, move into the kill zone of an attacker and drive the knife as hard as possible into the upper abdomen. Keeping a tight grip, preferably the hatchet grip, drop your weight and drive the blade down as hard as you can while it is still inside the body. You have just committed hara-kari for the assailant. The same technique could be committed in reverse (upward), or virtually at any angle you want after insertion.

METHODS OF ATTACK

There are infinite ways you may attack and defend. Some attacks are more effective and cunning than others but, in most scenarios, the best attack is the one that works. The two most common methods of attack we will focus on are direct and indirect. Direct attacks rely on economy of motion and speed, attacking the intended target without telegraph or deviation. Indirect attacks are tricks designed to deceive a defender of your real intentions and draw his defenses away from your real target.

DIRECT ATTACK

The simplest method of attack is the direct assault. Cutting the response line on your attacker, you blast at him in quick step, striking the closest available target. A series of direct attacks form a swarm in which you might literally climb up the attacker's limb, guard or body to his vitals. Keep your techniques rapid and economical, slashing and stabbing anything you can reach.

THE SECRET OF SIGHT ALIGNMENT

What I am about to tell you will change your ability forever. It will revolutionize your thinking on the art of striking. One day early on in my martial arts career, I heard of a fencing club. From my reading, I was familiar with fencing, and I knew that it was a major ingredient to Bruce Lee's Jeet Kune do, so I was interested in learning it. I was pretty cocky at the time, having never been beaten in the street or in sparring. When I entered the club my attitude was, "Okay, just teach me the basics and I'll whip all your butts," which is pretty much what happened. I was in top shape, fast, strong and quick on my feet, so I took to it like a duck in water. My long reach didn't hurt either. I'm over six feet and 200 pounds. In sparring I had defeated everyone, even guys that had been

Direct attacks are simple actions that make no attempt to hide thier intentions but instead rely heavily on speed and suddeness for thier effect.

The principle is simple, attack the closet target with the closest tool and get out of there.

An entire fight could be effectively won by the execution of a continous series of fast, direct attacks. Never underestimate speed and simplicity of action, they are the foundation of combative skill.

there for years. They didn't like me much, but I wasn't there for a popularity contest. I was there to learn how to fence.

I beat everyone, everyone that is except the Mystro (French fencing lingo for master teacher), who promptly turned me into a human pin cushion. It seemed that every time I moved to attack, I was struck suddenly with the tip of the sword. I never saw it coming, much to my dismay and the joy of the other students. It was a humbling experience as I realized that if it were a real duel, I'd be dead.

For the first time in my life I had a new motto: you beat me, you teach me. I humbly requested that he instruct me in the finer points of the art of the foil. I don't think he liked me much, and back then I can't say I blame him, but after much convincing, he agreed to take me on as a private student. For months the art of fencing become my focus. I learned as much as I could about the foil and the saber, its history and intricacies. I attended every class I could. I asked every question, and sought out and read every book on the subject I could find. I even went so far as to rent old Errol Flynn movies and play them back frame by frame on my VCR. It was fun, but in the school my own personal history kept repeating itself. Every time I talked the instructor into a bout, he would kill me - every time. It was driving me crazy. Here I was, younger, stronger, faster, bigger and I thought more cunning, yet every time we fought he seemed to get the jump on me. I couldn't see his attacks coming until it was too late.

Then one day I had a revelation that changed my view of combat forever. I was standing off to the side talking to one of the assistant instructors when the Mystro began to spar another student on the other side of the room. As I watched, it hit me like a ton of bricks. What he was doing and what he was

teaching were two different things. It was so simple and subtle, but to me it was a revelation. He would change his blade position just before he struck. Before he attacked you, he would raise the blade slightly and align it with your eyesight. To this day I don't know if he even knew he was doing it. Why did this make a difference you ask? Well imagine that I have a 2x4 inch piece of pine four feet long. And let's say I swing it at you right to left across the horizon. What you'll see is a large piece of wood coming at you from the side – big, wide, visible and easy to block.

On the other hand, let's say instead of swinging it at you, I point it at you. I align it up with your eyes, and pop you with it like a pool que. In this scenario, you see only the end of the board (2x4 inches) and its length remains hidden. Same piece of wood in each situation, but when you align it with someone's eyesight, you effectively distort his depth perception. And in the sum total of all the motions occurring in combat, that's not much to see.

That's what my fencing instructor was doing and when I understood it, he never beat me again. Since I have applied the concept of sight alignment to striking, specifically my jab, no one has stopped my attacks. I took the concept of distorting my opponent's perception and began to apply it to everything I could. In the area of knife fighting, it can be exceptionally brutal and effective. Imagine a strike that's lightning fast and comes out of nowhere. Now imagine a spike on the end of that strike, and you will begin to see how devastating this concept can be with weapons. Now I give this knowledge to you.

THE PERFECT STRIKE

The act of sight alignment should be used whenever you need to attack with your

One of the most important secrets of the art of Dynamic Combat is the sight alignment principle. Sight alignment is the act of aligning your strike directly with the opponent's line of vision, thereby diminishing the visible mass in delivery and distorting his depth perception. Imagine you are facing a fencer. The first time he engages you, he comes at you with blade lowered. In this position you can see much of the length of the blade and have a good chance of recognizing its motion. The second time he engages you, he raises his weapon and aligns it with your eyes, thus distorting your perception of both its length and motion.

The Dynamic Combat jab and speed stab utilize sight alignment to create an almost invisible initial strike.

fastest and most effective strike. Use it at the inception of a fight or when you need results right now. When you have to take another person out, you must first enter his kill zone, a place where you could also be dropped. Therefore, the action you take must have the most immediate effect possible, which brings us to the Dynamic Combat speed stab.

THE SPEED STAB

The speed stab is the fastest, longest and most perfect strike you have in this system. It is quick, economical and sight-aligned. If launched from just outside the kill zone without telegraphing your intentions, your opponent will not even see it until it's too late.

To execute, adopt your Dynamic Combat knife fighting stance. Cut the response line and get as close as you can without inviting retaliation by your opponent. Keeping yourself compact and your defense tight, align the blade (and your forearm) up with the attacker's eyesight. Keep the elbow down and to your side. Now, without telegraphing, explode forward driving the point of the blade along his line of sight, striking him in the eyes or face. The body and the blade should move simultaneously. If done correctly, it should catch your opponent by surprise. From this point, you can flow into another attack, reposition on him or escape.

One of the most unique and devastating concepts in the art of Dynamic Combat is offensive sight alignment. It is the ability to distort an opponents perception of an incoming attack through the perfect alignment of the strike with his line of vision.

INDIRECT ATTACK

An indirect attack is another way to say fake. Put simply, a fake is a physical lie you tell an attacker designed to hide your real intentions. Fakes offer a method of deception that can be deployed if your direct attacks aren't working. The best fakes draw an opponent's defenses away from his vital targets and momentarily create an opening for your real attack. The secrets to a good fake are a good sense of timing and an awareness of your opponent's individual response patterns. For example, a nervous or jittery fighter will often overreact to the slightest gesture on your part. Against this type of person you must use quick, short fakes. On the other hand, with a calm, focused fighter you must almost strike him to get him to react.

To fake an attacker, extend the response line giving both you and him more time to react. Once you've got your attacker's attention (by an attack or the threat of one), execute a strike to an area you wish to draw him to. One caution though: the fake must look like a real strike. To be effective your opponent must believe that you are really trying to get him. Make your strikes fast and threatening, exaggerating the action slightly. As your fake strike reaches approximately halfway to extension, change direction and strike as fast as you can to your real target as your opponent defends your initial movement. If you score a hit, follow up with a swarm before he can recover. If it is unsuccessful, begin mixing up direct and indirect attacks and take advantage of his confusion.

An indirect attack is a physical lie you tell your opponent. The idea is to bait the attacker into placing himself in a position of vulnerability.

Here the attacker deceives his opponent by attacking low into the abdomen. He strikes out with a quick, threatening stab tot he stomach which draws the defender to perform a sudden low-line defensive action.

When the opponent reacts to block, the attacker changes his line of attack to the upper body.

ATTACKS FROM THE SABER

Because of the natural precision the grip provides, attacking from the saber should be your primary offensive and defensive strategy. Attacks from this grip should emphasize the full extension of your reach by attacking the closest target from the farthest distance. Mix up your attacks by using both slashes and stabs, or more advanced cuts, taking care not to exaggerate or expose yourself in the process.

The saber grip is often referred to as the surgical grip because of the amount of dexterity it affords.

It is a natural and effective grip and should be your primary method of holding and deploying the blade.

ATTACKS FROM THE ICE PICK

When utilizing the ice pick strategy, you should make one minor modification to the Dynamic Combat knife fighting stance. Since most of your actions will be downward onto the attacker's guard or into his throat, upper body and head, raise the blade arm in front of you, much like a boxer. Don't overextend. Perhaps the most common mistake when attacking from this position is unnecessary exaggeration. All other body positions remain the same. Keep you actions tight and streamlined. Slashes should be in tight, small circles, no more than is necessary, returning to a tight guard quickly. The same is true with all stabbing actions.

Attacking from the ice pick or blade down position is designed to overwhelm and control an attacker. If you are in a confined space and/or don't have much time, this tactic can be devastating. Although I wouldn't fight with it against another knife fighter, especially at a distance, this attack is great in most other situations, provided you have the required speed and coordination to pull it off.

All grips other than the saber are utilized for a distinct tactical advantage they may give you.

Here, Ryan decides to change tactics. He rotates the blade forward toward his opponent...

... and cuts the response line in preparation for a sudden ice pick attack.

Suddenly, Ryan explodes with a punch-like strike slashing the attacker's lead arm with great speed and force.

In the same motion he flows forward slashing his opponent twice with the same attack. A non-lethal vartiation of this attack would be to strike with the fist to the face with the second action instead of slashing the attackers throat.

ATTACKS FROM THE HATCHET

Anytime you grip the knife in the palm of your hand like a fist (knife handle at a right angle to the hand), you have a very strong grip. This strong, stable position is one of the greatest advantages of both ice pick and hatchet grips. So when you really need to strike hard or make sure you maintain control of your blade, it's advisable to switch grip positions.

While the ice pick grip provides a "praying mantis-like" downward control of your attacker, the hatchet grip does the opposite. It is ideal for cutting upward and attacking the flanks in close. Although it can be used like the saber, it is best to utilize traps and cuts that come upward or around the side of centerline. In addition, because of its natural grip strength, it's a good gripping platform for power cuts and hacking techniques. Like the ice pick, it is also important not to exaggerate your actions.

The hatchet grip is simple and stronger than the saber position because the thumb can wrap around the handle for greater support. This greater strength can be utilized in trapping and slashing attacks to maximum effect.

Here Ryan slips from saber to hatchet without his opponent noticing. He rotates the blade in his hand so it is facing toward him and lashes out, catching the opponent's arm and removing it from the guard position.

Ryan continues by trapping the rising arm, preventing his opponent from blocking.

Once vulnerable, he attacks the lower body with power stabs.

Regardless of what type of grip you use, always make sure you hold onto the weapon tightly. Most people don't realize how easy the knife can be dislodged from the hand on contact. Regardless of the grip, make sure you hold the weapon tightly or you may lose it at the point of first contact.

CHAPTER EIGHT

DEFENSE AND COUNTERATTACK

"Resistance is what separates reality from fantasy."

– Richard Ryan

The art of defense and counterattack with the blade is an exact science. In a knife fight, you must be able to protect yourself from the attacker's blade and simultaneously deliver decisive attacks of your own, and you must do so without any mistakes. Sounds easy, but it is not. The main problem is that the blade is a high speed touch weapon. Because of the lack of need for physical strength, attacks and counters can happen in a fraction of a second, making the knife the fastest close quarter battle tool in the world.

Unlike the movies, real fights seldom go down exactly as you want them to. There are too many variables. Murphy's Law is always, I repeat, always in effect. You can't control exactly when or how an attacker may come at you. In fact, the only thing you can control is yourself and your reaction to what happens. Victory goes to the fighter who has the best position and techniques and who can adapt to the ever changing situation without hesitation, and to the fighter with the best luck.

UNDERSTANDING REACTION TIME

The techniques of defense and counterattack are more difficult skill sets than the art of attack. This is because they are considerably more complicated, requiring greater awareness and connection to an opponent's actions. A good attack requires timing, speed and accuracy, but not in the same degree that an act of defense and counterattack does. To explain this, let's go through each process by comparison.

An attack can be blind in which you just lash out, hoping to catch something, usually in an act of desperation and fear, or it can be subjective in the sense that you choose when, how and where you strike based on the actions or inactions of your opponent. Only amateurs or the "soon to be dead" lash out blindly in a knife fight. We'll assume you're not one of those and discuss the premeditated timed attack.

Your opponent circles you, threatening with his blade. He sticks it in your face, thrusting it at you, trying to intimidate you by fear. When he presents it again, you determine the relative position of his limb (your target), and you whip out your blade, catching him solidly on the muscles of the upper arm, cutting him to the bone and causing him to drop his weapon. The speed and efficiency of your action caught him by surprise and it shows in the look of shock and pain that flushes his face. This technique is simple, fast and efficient, and not that difficult to achieve against someone like this.

On the other hand, let's say the attacker circles you again. This time, he stays tight and compact, keeping a healthy distance from your blade. He makes his body small and mobile. In other words, he offers no real targets. Suddenly, he advances into the kill zone in quick step and unleashes an attack of his own. Now things have gotten much more complicated. First of all, you must not only determine what type of attack it is (linear or circular), but where it is going to strike (high, middle, low, inside or outside lines, etc.). Once you know this, you must now evade or intercept the attack before it reaches its destination. This means exact and unforgiving timing. Top that off with the possibility that he attacks more than once in a single advance, and the need to launch a counterattack of your own to an open target and, congratulations, you've reached a much higher level of complexity. Even if performed with a cooperative partner in slow motion, this is much too advanced for most people without exact and proper training. Cram all this into the space of a few deadly seconds, and you begin to understand why the art of the counterattack is lost on most people when challenged by anyone but a cooperative partner or an instructor in a pre-choreographed demonstration.

Complexity aside, the art of defense and counter has its own advantages. First, whenever someone attacks you, he is open to counterattack somewhere. An attacker must leave the confines of a protective stance and distance, and enter into the opponent's kill zone and extends a limb, even if just for a moment. The great fighters know this and will draw out a less experienced fighter to his doom. They will lull him into thinking he is in control or intimidate him as he retreats from the assault. When the amateur

becomes more bold or committed to a finishing assault, he is dropped by a sudden interception in the middle of his advance. This is called a stop hit – striking as the assailant attacks you. Like gunfighters of old, a professional can draw and hit first, even when the attacker launches his attack first. Much of this ability comes from mastering the art of defense and counter. The point is that counterattack is a precise skill that requires superior technique and timing.

THE TIME/DISTANCE VARIABLE

In combat, distance must be defined according to the concept of time. The time/distance variable is a simple concept I created to convey an understanding of the relationship between the two. Put simply, the more distance you have between you and your attacker, the more time you have to react. The less distance, the less time. In other words, the closer the threat, the faster things will occur and vice versa. The control of range becomes a vital factor in your ability to react and respond to whatever an attacker does. No matter what your skill level, if you let an opponent get too close, you can be overwhelmed before you know what has happened. This is one of the most critical concepts you must understand and control if you are to win a knife fight. You must control distance so you have time to react.

THE KILL ZONE

A person standing within arms' reach of you (or closer) is in your kill zone. We call it the kill zone because you can easily be killed when someone is this close to you. At this distance, you have little or no time to react to an attack, especially if it is fast and non-telegraphic. The hands are quicker than the eye (just ask any magician) and, at this range, a quick person can strike you before you can see it coming. With or without a weapon, everyone is dangerous at arm's reach. As a

general rule, never let a potentially hostile person in the kill zone, at least not for long, or without some action on your part.

THE ATTACK ZONE

The attack zone is defined as arms' reach plus one step away. It is called this because this is the most common distance within which an attack will occur. Most often, an assailant will negotiate to conversational range - not too close where you can clock him, and not too far where his attack will be too slow, but at a distance at which he can take one quick step and get to you. But by keeping an opponent in the attack zone, you have doubled the distance and therefore doubled your reaction time, a.k.a. the time/distance variable. No matter how swift and non-telegraphic his strikes may be, he must telegraph his attack with a full step.

THE DANGER ZONE

The last range is the danger zone. Instead of defining range by increments such as punching range, kicking range, grappling range, stickfighting range, gunfighting range etc., it makes more sense to define the kill and attack zones and include all other ranges as "danger zones." Technically, the danger zone is two or more steps away from the kill zone. But it could be three steps or thirty. It makes no difference. Anyone within your immediate area is a possible threat in a hostile situation and, in a crisis, you should be prepared to take action at anytime against anyone at any distance.

THE TIME/DISTANCE RULE

After defining what is meant by the time/distance variable and defining the three ranges of combat, we need to now incorporate them into a usable and easy to remember rule of thumb. The time/distance

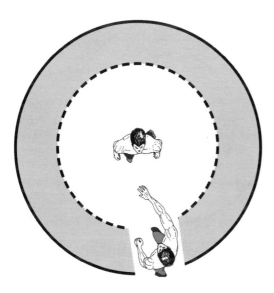

ATTACK ZONE

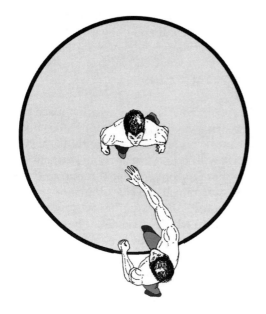

In most violent situations distance is your friend. Distance equals reaction time, providing us with critical seconds we need to deal with sudden attack. The three zone concept is a simple way to control range and reaction time without too much thought.

Kill Zone is the distance at which you or an attacker can reach out and touch the other without having to take a step. The attack zone is kill zone range plus one full step back. The danger zone is two or more steps away.

KILL ZONE

It is important to view the zone concepts as a 360 degree sphere of influence around your body at all times, not just the area in front of you. In a hostile situation you are in danger from anyone within your immediate proximity.

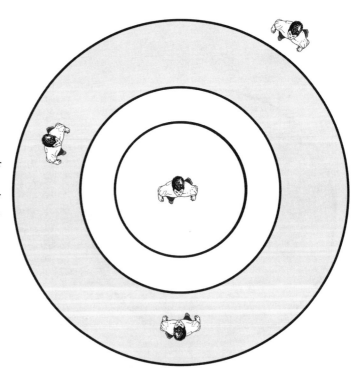

DANGER ZONE

rule is more of a reminder than a rule. It states that in combat you'll always need more time and more distance than you think you do. Remember that you should never underestimate anyone. That fat guy might be quicker on his feet than you imagined, and that skinny guy may be hyper aggressive and able to overwhelm you with sudden force. Fueled by the powers of adrenaline and determination, someone who is woefully inadequate physically could become the last person you see on the planet as he punches, kicks, cuts, slashes or otherwise beats you into oblivion, all in the space of a few deadly seconds. Always assume that anyone can explode on you in a fraction of a second or less. Don't let yourself get sucker punched (or stabbed) by underestimating how fast someone can cover the distance and attack you. When threatened, anticipation of sudden attack will go a long way to keeping you from being the victim. Always remember that in combat, distance is your friend. Burn that into your mind. With distance comes reaction time. The more reaction time, the more likely I will be able to deal with the attacker and his

attack. This is true with or without weapons, but especially with the sharp pointed kind. You should never let any attacker with a blade into the kill zone without some reaction. Your first response should be quick footwork, repositioning yourself for your own attack or counter. If the encounter is not in the "kill or be killed" stage yet, at very least get your hands up into a confrontation management position allowing you to protect your vitals against sudden attack. If it becomes a fight, use your footwork to sprint out of the kill zone. If possible, give him something to remember you by for daring to step into your space. As a general rule, if someone attacks you, cut or slash anything you can reach and increase your distance as much as possible.

SEEING IS NOT PERCEIVING

There is a difference between seeing something and perceiving it. Sight is in the eyes and perception is in the mind. The eyes are just the cameras for your brain. If you think about it, your ability to process information about your situation, the attacker and perhaps his attack itself is the first and most important skill in combat. Without accurate perception, all is lost. You can't stop what you can't see.

Think of the eyes like a video camera. Like the camera, they record images for the brain to interpret. If you put the camera on wide angle, point it directly at the attacker and hold it steady, the image you record will be clear. Play it back and anyone would be able to pick out the details easily. On the other hand, imagine that you zoom in on the attacker's face. Doing so, you'll miss everything he does with his limbs and body. Watch his hands, and you lose his feet. Zoom in on his body and limbs and you'll miss his buddy stepping into the picture to his side. If your attacker makes a move and you violently shake the camera and flash or cover the lens momentarily with one hand, what will you see in the playback? Nothing recognizable. Yet this is exactly how most people react in a fight. They focus on

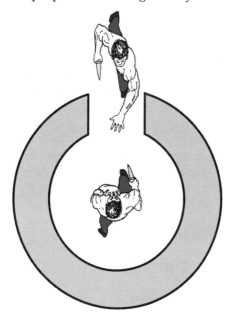

one thing to the exclusion of others. I train S.W.A.T. teams and law enforcement agencies and therefore I am given the opportunity to participate in a wide variety of their training and schools. I have attended various schools that use video simulators with both live and simulated fire. In this type of training, a scenario unfolds in front of you. You respond to a robbery, domestic violence, murder or other situation, playing to the scenario on a big screen in front of you. It's great training. Often the bad guys draw down on you and you have to fire to survive. When the scenario is over, the computer can play back where your shots hit and even where your barrel was pointed at any given time. This is important because it is an indication of where you're looking. It amazed me how many times people shot the bad guy's weapon. Under stress, tunnel vision kicks in and most people fixate on the greatest danger. They stare at the weapon. They shut their eyes. They flinch or turn away when attacked.

Unfortunately, this is exactly opposite of what you must do. Remember you can't stop what you can't see. For you to be able to take any valid action you must see what you're dealing with. The more clearly you see it, the more precisely you will be able to respond. In training or in combat, teach yourself not to blink. Don't flinch. Don't turn away. Force yourself to look potentially lethal force in the eye and deal with it. Focus your vision somewhere around the opponent's chest without excluding your focus on his limbs or your surroundings. From the chest, you can see his every movement. You'll see a direct attack with his hands. You'll see him shift his weight to kick. You'll see him load a power strike. If he is unarmed, his hands are his most dangerous weapons. Be aware of their position at all times without taking your vision from his chest. With a weapon in hand, it is the weapon itself that is most dangerous. Track its movements with your mind's eye at every moment but don't look at it directly. Doing so will tend to make you over-focus on the weapon much like zooming in with the video camera. Do so and a cunning fighter will clock you with the hand or foot you're not watching. When the action starts, don't shrink from it. Closing your eyes or turning away will not make the attacker disappear. It will only put you in a perceptual disadvantage. Train yourself to keep your eyes open during even the most vicious battles and you have a much greater chance of survival.

MINDSET

Okay, you understand the role of time, distance and vision in combat. We've discussed perceptual issues. Now it's time to deal with your thought process during a violent conflict. Remember that any weapon is a tool. Whether simple like a rock or a stick, or more complex like a semiautomatic handgun, it is still just a tool. Before you can master any tool, you must first become the user of the tool. The mind controls the body;

the body controls the tools. Without proper mindset the deadliest warrior with the deadliest weapon will be dead in his tracks. An inferior foe with inferior weapons but a ruthless and focused state of mind will win every time. Ultimately it is you that is the real weapon, and the power to wield this weapon all starts in your head.

PERCEPTION AND THE MIND

The study of Zen teaches to live in the moment, and in reality it's all we really have, the here and now. At this moment, you sit there reading my words on this page. As you pass each word it ceases to exist as another takes its place again and again like the flow of water in a river. Your stream of consciousness deciphers the text, absorbs it and moves on. Stop reading and your stream of consciousness takes you on another journey, perhaps one of internal thought or reflection as you contemplate what you have read. We exist in the fleeting moment. The past is gone the moment it is experienced and the future has yet to happen. This is the way it should be. The way it is. It is the way of the master. If you want to master the arts of war, you must learn to live in the moment. You must learn not to anticipate what may be or grasp at what was. You must deal only in the present, moment by moment, second by second. To do this, you must be willing to accept and deal with the cold reality of your situation, no matter how grave it may be. This is something many people say they can do, but few have the stomach for when it comes right down to it.

To illustrate the importance of this, let's say you are cornered in an alley by a big ugly thug. In fact, he's the stereotypical big ugly thug. He's 250 pounds of sweaty, smelly biker scum. He comes fully equipped with the colors, tattoos and scars minus a neck. He stands 20 feet from you, blocking your exit. "I heard of you," he spits. "You that knife guy. Well, I'm gonna show ya a few tricks you ain't never seen." With that, he reaches into his boot and pulls the meanest, longest looking bowie knife you've ever laid eyes on. A glint of the steel catches the street light. So does his gold tooth as he smiles a wicked smile. "I'm gonna gut you like a fish," he says, sounding like Clint Eastwood. He crouches slightly and begins to move at you slowly, slicing the air in a figure eight pattern.

Most people would swallow their tongue and empty their bowels in this situation. The overload of fear and adrenaline taps into the emotional side of the brain, dumping thoughts of pain and suffering into our consciousness. We imagine what is going to happen to us. This emotional overload (not the biker) is what gets most people killed. They panic when it is critical that they remain calm and collected.

Our minds, our "bio-computers," store thoughts, images and emotions. In fact, everything we have ever thought, felt or experienced is in there somewhere. When faced with an extremely dangerous situation, the undisciplined mind begins to lose it. We lose control of the flow of our thoughts. Our minds become clouded with unnecessary things which clutter our perception and distort our decision-making processes. We become caught in a web of our own making. This is a web made of fear and emotion that affects our ability to live in the moment and deal with our immediate problems.

Imagine that you hear a siren right now. Take a second and think about it. When you hear a siren, what comes to mind? A police car? A fire truck? A car accident? You imagined something, didn't you? That is how your mind works. You digest a stimulus which triggers a thought process brought about by your life experiences. If you're a cop and you hear a siren, you think of cops. A person whose house burned down once will probably think of a fire truck. This is the way we think. But in combat, this is an incorrect and dangerous thought process. If you heard a siren right now, the only physical reality is the sound waves that hit your ears. The images it provokes are not real. There are no fire trucks or police cars in the room as you read this book. They are a figment of your imagination and they have no place in a fight.

So let's get back to our ugly friend. Remembering that physical realities are the only thing that matters, let's revisit the situation. On the surface, it seem that we are being threatened and intimidated by a biker. His image scares us. His words scare us and his weapon scares us. But the reality is that he is a large, probably strong human being who has threatened you. He has an edged weapon in his right hand and is moving it in a clockwise figure eight pattern. He is moving at you slowly from 20 feet. Eighteen. Sixteen. Fourteen. The point I'm trying to make is that actions are the only thing that matter. All the details, the way he looks, what he says, etc., have no bearing on the fight. Think of the situation like a computer would, in cold rational terms. Erase the opponent's face, his clothing, and his words, and just deal with his actions and you have acquired the combat mindset. Your best chance of survival is to become ruthlessly calm and viciously calculating and turn off your emotions. You can deal with them later, after you've dealt with the attacker. Focus 100 percent of your attention on what the attacker is doing or trying to do every moment of the fight. Don't blink, don't flinch, and don't let emotional overload dominate the situation. Focus completely on his actions and you'll react when and how you need to.

TO CUT OR NOT TO CUT

In any self-defense situation, the best defense is not to be there in the first place. Avoidance

and escape are protection based on higher intelligence. But alas there are times in which this is not possible and you have to stay and fight for your life or the innocent life of someone else. But that does not mean you have to stand toe-to-toe with your assailant and punch or slash it out to the bitter end. Even in a relatively confined space, a fighter with quick footwork and evasive skills can move, as to avoid contact with an attacker much of the time and, when edged weapons are involved, this is just plain common sense. Being human, we all make mistakes, and Murphy's Law is always in effect. The last thing you want to do is stand and trade blows with knives. Therefore, evasive footwork should become your first and foremost method of defense. If an attacker cannot reach you, it matters not how strong, fast or tough he is (or how sharp his blade is). Remember the time/distance rule - you always need more time and more distance than you think you do - and adjust your tactics accordingly. Whenever possible, keep your distance and let your attacker commit to trying to catch you. When he's open, or overcommits himself, strike.

EVASIVE ACTION

The specific techniques of avoiding and evading any attack are numerous and complicated. They are too complex to be taught effectively in a book. What can be easily transferred is the concept of evasion. Avoiding danger is a natural and instinctive act. It is wired into our central nervous system. For example, you are out for a stroll and suddenly a bird swoops from the side and flies by your head. What do you do? You duck, that's what. As a matter of fact, almost everyone on the planet would have ducked too. You duck without conscious thought because this reaction is wired into the human nervous system and there for our protection. These same instinctive reactions can and should be applied in combat. Say an attacker suddenly slashes close to your face. It startles you and you snap your head and throat back with the attack and step out of range. That is a good evasion, simple, natural and reactive. The trick is not to overdo it. Due to the hard wiring of the evasion impulse, almost anyone can evade with great speed, especially when startled. But most people overreact. They let the evasion go too far and find themselves off balance or out of position. In this case the attacker needs only follow-up his initial attack to score a decisive hit. Use your natural instinct to evade. Don't suppress it, but don't allow yourself to lose control of your balance or your positioning. Maintain the ability to strike back at any time.

BLOCKS, PARRIES AND SHIELDS

A block stops an incoming strike force against force. A parry deflects the strike by impacting it at a right angle and deflecting it away from its intended target. Both blocks and parries use some area of your body that is less susceptible to injury such as the forearm, elbow, hand or leg. You need both methods of defense because which one you use is really not up to you. Your attacker decides which is the most appropriate technique. For example, straight blows and stabs are usually parried. However, you can't parry a wide curricular punch or slash; you have to stop it. But the real problem with blocks and parries isn't this decision making process, but the fact that each of them requires perfect timing to work. This is something most people don't have. This realization gave birth to the invention of the shielding concept. Shields have been used in war throughout history. The concept is simple. A shield provides a strong barrier against the assault by simply putting something in the way of the attack, stopping it from breaking through to a vital target. It covers the vitals and protects them regardless of whether the attack is linear or circular. The drawback is that you are absorbing punishment, no doubt about it, but it is not intended to be used like Mohammed

Ali's rope-a-dope. You don't stand there and let someone slash, stab or pound on you until he gets tired. You use a shield when you must and counter or move instantly.

Years ago when I began to develop my knife fighting system, I began by looking at all existing systems. One of the greatest weaknesses I found was in the stances they adopted and the methods of defense. All of them utilized attacking with the knife. That's the easy part, but they lacked realism in other areas. That is why I created my combat crouch with the guard hand vertical on the centerline of the body. This position not only offered maximum protection, but provided a constant shield for the vitals along the vertical line of the upper torso. Worst case, if you were to trade with another knife fighter whose centerline is not protected, it's highly likely that you would be the winner simply because your position is superior. You have a shield. This is not to imply that you don't ever block or parry an attack. The general rule is that you block or parry blows that are slower or telegraphic. But when the action gets fast and furious, it's better to stay tight and compact and shield the attacks. The shield is the safest of all blocking-type actions because it remains in place. The problem with it is that you absorb punishment, and if that punishment is a razor sharp knife, you can't absorb much. Because of this, the shielding in a knife fight should be used as a last resort, when you cannot move or the attacker gets the jump on you and is right on top of you in the kill zone slashing away. Shield and move. This is not a good thing; so try to avoid having to use it with good footwork.

BLOCKING WITH THE BLADE

I cannot stress enough that good footwork is essential to mastering the art of knife fighting. With good footwork you can keep all your vital targets out of reach. When a attacker lunges, you can retreat at equal

Evasion is the art of not being there when you're attacked. Although it is a science, it is important to keep it instinctive.

Here an attacker lunges with a wild attack. The defender snaps his body back, away from the direction of the strike…

…and retaliates before the attacker can recover his balance and position. It is instinctive to avoid contact with an attacker's blade. Learn to use these instincts to your advantage by incorporating evasive movements into your offensive and defensive technique.

Although evasion is a superior form of defense, there are times when you have no choice but to stop an incoming attack. If you have to block, it is important that you do it right. The most common mistake people make when blocking is to overcommit and exaggerate their movements. Here John demonstrates incorrect blocking technique.

He reaches out far beyond the body line putting too much motion and energy into his defenses.

Another common mistake is to move or drop the defensive hand away from the body during motion. If you open yourself up, you will be cut.

Here John demonstrates the correct method of blocking and parrying incoming attacks.

He keeps his guard up, protecting his body from attack at all times during the block. He blocks only as much as is necessary, keeping the action within body lines to avoid overcommitment and exposure.

Take the time to practice your blocks in a mirror. This can be very helpful in finding quirks and flaws in motion you never knew existed. Pay close attention to form. Stay compact and tight and move as fast as you can.

distance and counter his attack. This is ideal because he can't get to your body, but you can get to his attacking limb. This brings us to the next point. Stay tight in your stance and use your knife for everything you can, both offense and defense, and try to keep your guard hand in place as much as possible. If you remove your guard hand to block or parry and miss, there is nothing to protect your vitals. On the other hand, if you keep your guard in place and use the knife to block, and you miss, the guard is still there. By using the knife to block, you are also doing damage. Defense becomes offense and it is possible to stop an attacker with a single slashing block which cuts deep into the attacking arm.

THE RESPONSE LINE

Another concept I developed years ago that has applied especially well to knife fighting is the idea of a response line. The response line is an imaginary line between you and your immediate adversary that serves as a kind of warning device. It is an imaginary line that, when crossed, demands a response. When your opponent crosses the response line you must either attack, counter or move. I realized early on that another instinctive sense we all have is the sense of proximity danger. We all know when a hostile person is too close to us. Our internal alarm signals go off when someone threatens us and moves into our space. Even without the obvious threat, we can sense when another person is too close for us to react in time. Try an experiment. Have someone stand about 15 feet from you. At this distance, you should feel pretty safe. Now imagine that he is a hostile threat and might attack you. Have him slowly move toward you a foot at a time. With each step your level of sensory anxiety will increase. As he begins to invade your personal space and close in on the kill zone, you should suddenly feel a little panicky. Now try it again. If you pay close attention,

there is a "line" somewhere inside the attack zone that he comes to where you instinctively want to move to avoid having him get too close. That is the response line. Use the instinctive sense of danger to help you maintain a reactive distance from an attacker. Because in a fight, you don't have time to measure distance. You can't be looking at the ground and saying, "I've got to keep six feet away." Most likely you will be occupied with more important matters. But you can use your instincts. Practice sensing the response line. Have a partner do footwork drills with you and develop your sense of the response line by letting your instincts tell you when he gets too close. Practice keeping him outside the line and it will be very hard for him to get to you.

CUT AND RUN

We've established that evasion is the best and first form of defense, especially in a knife fight. It just so happens that it is also the number one tactical response. In most situations in which you have a reasonable amount of time to see the situation coming, your first tactic should be to cut and run. The concept is simple. Cut anything that you can reach or anything that enters your attack zone and retreat, repeating the process.

If you have the space and the speed of foot to do this, it can be a very effective method of winning a knife fight. If you can keep your vital targets outside the attacker's reach and cut him when he attacks you, he will be forced to make a decision rather quickly. He may decide that it isn't worth it as his blood decorates the ground. He may turn and flee. If he doesn't, you may get lucky with a strike and de-fang him, forcing him to drop his weapon. He may panic or increase his commitment to get to you and expose himself in the process. When he over-commits, you can deliver a decisive counterattack.

Cut and run applies to both attack and counterattack tactics. You can take the initiative and go after the adversary cutting whatever you can reach and keeping your distance…

…or you can wait till he attacks you…

…move with his attack and out of range, cutting as you leave.

To cut and run, shorten your base of support and raise your center of gravity slightly so it will be easier for you to move quickly. You need to realize though that someone can run forwards faster than you can run backwards. We don't have any world class backwards running sprinters, so be ready and keep as much distance between you as possible. Let him do the attacking while you whittle away at anything you can reach.

CUT AND STAY

The second tactic is cut and stay. Cut and stay is often used when you cannot move effectively because you may be injured or the logistics of the situation don't allow you the space to move. With this tactic, your objective is to stand your ground, stop your attacker cold and deliver a decisive attack or counter. As stated before, I don't recommend that you spend much time in the kill zone trading strikes with knives, so even if you are forced to use this tactic, your primary objective is to get away as soon as you can.

To effectively cut and stay you must be able to deliver one or more telling blows within the shortest possible time frame. As a general rule, it is wise to use quick, powerful linear stabs to center mass. The more the better. The only exception to this rule is if the attacker leaves an obvious target open that requires another attack, such as the throat, which would be better attacked with a deep, powerful slash.

Whenever you cut and stay, it's wise to adjust your positioning, especially if

The key to cut and run is to stay out of the attacker's kill zone. To do this, keep your distance and use your reach to extend your cutting radius.

you have the time. If possible, switch sides, placing the blade hand and foot back. This position emphasizes the use of the guard hand as a shield arm, putting it out in front of you where you can utilize it to stop, block and trap the incoming attack. It's also wise to anticipate a possible collision. His body may collide with you when you engage at kill zone. This means having a drive leg, a wide base of support and a low center of gravity. Lastly, get small. As a matter of fact, in this situation you cannot be too small. Regardless of your actual physical size, crouch as much as possible and keep the entire body compact. When the opponent closes, drive into him, shielding or grabbing his attacking limb with the guard, while simultaneously counterstriking as quickly and as many times as you can before you break away and recover. If you are attacked suddenly or by a confusing assault you cannot track or decipher, drop into cut and stay and launch a series of piston-like counterstabs to centermass. Chances are you will be effective and he will not.

CUT AND KILL

When developing my tactics I looked for a more politically correct name than cut and kill, which happens to be the third primary knife strategy in my system. I decided to keep the name because it says exactly what

Cut and stay is a tactic you should use when you are forced to stand your ground or you chose to do so to finish the conflict.

Here Ryan transitions from blade forward to blade back position and stabilizes himself for the collision.

The attacker lunges with a powerful downward stab to the Ryan's face. Instead of retreating, Ryan takes the opposite tactic, moving directly into the assault and bracing himself for impact...

...becoming smaller and more compact on contact and delivering a series of power stabs to center mass.

Cut and stay is risky business. You must either have great composure and skill or a lot of luck. I suggest you don't count on the luck part and take the time to practice defending against all types of close range assaults without the luxury of movement.

In any case, when cut and stay you must be instantly effective with your counterattack. The longer the collision lasts the greater the chance of injury or mistakes. Strike hard and direct and end the encounter immediately.

this strategy is. In this mode, your objective is to take the fight to your attacker and finish him off as quickly as possible. To even consider cut and kill tactics, you should have tried everything you can to avoid and escape the situation. Having exhausted all other options, you are now forced into more drastic action. In other words, you have no other option but to try to incapacitate or kill your attacker as quickly as you can. The extreme danger of a knife fight aside, a situation which may warrant this tactic as an initial response may be one in which you are protecting a loved one who may be injured or killed. Perhaps you are faced with multiple attackers, or a single attacker with a superior weapon such as a handgun. In any case, you are forced to use the extremes of your survival tactics.

Before we get into the technical aspects of cut and kill, it needs to be said that the suddenness of your attack and the element of surprise are by far the two most important factors. Regardless of the technique deployed, an attacker who explodes on his victim with tremendous speed and fury can overwhelm even the most prepared fighter. The rule is that when you are forced to attack, you do so without hesitation and with merciless resolve.

TRAP AND ATTACK

A trap is a temporary immobilization of an attacker's guard, hand or limb. It allows you a moment in which he cannot defend or counter and you can deliver your strike. In fencing terms, it is the act of attacking the blade, beating it aside and delivering a thrust of your own. When you fence with the smaller swords, the guard hand can pave the way for your blade in the same manner. Although forms of trapping are many and varied, it's best to keep it simple and work with the concept. When the opportunity presents itself, explode forward into the kill zone reaching out and checking, pressing or

knocking your opponent's guard aside, and simultaneously strike. If you can continue to hold and check, do so. If you lose him, recover your guard hand and continue your assault.

GETTING AN ANGLE

Cut and kill often includes a technique called cut and pass. Sounding more like a football play than a knife tactic, cut and pass is a method of attempting to get an angle of advantage on an opponent. When attacking, you engage your attacker directly, then suddenly veer off centerline as much as possible while trapping his limbs, cutting through defenses. Depending on your momentum and the type of attack, you may even spin off-line with your blade following a lethal tornado-like path. This tactic is best deployed against a stationary or aggressive opponent. As a matter of fact, one of its best uses is against a fast rushing assault. When an attacker rushes you, he picks up momentum. The faster he moves, and the heavier he is, the harder it is for him to stop or change direction quickly. You can take advantage of this by side stepping his assault and countering off-line. But it's difficult to do against someone who is retreating constantly, because the attacker can adjust his centerline while backing up. Remember that any angle off of centerline is an advantage. When you move in for the cut and kill, try to get an angle on your opponent and overwhelm him with more strikes than he can handle.

These three tactics, "cut and run", "cut and stay" and "cut and kill" are the defensive and counter offensive foundation of the system. In the end, you run your own war. You are free to deploy any tactic any time you wish. But the smart fighter will use cut and run as much as possible unless and until it is obvious that another tactic will be more effective. In a knife fight, it is always better to be safe than sorry and cut and run affords the safest strategy.

Cut and kill is the art of attack and it be used any time during the conflict. If the attacker is tentative or hesitant to commit, you can still block and counter from the blade back position.

In most situations is wise to use Cut and Run or Cut and Stay tactics at the outset of the encounter. However, you should always be ready to pounce on the attacker at the first sign of hesitation or weakness. Stay away from his blade and cut anything he puts into the kill zone.

When you get a reaction or the attacker hesitates...

...attack! Don't give him the time or opportunity to recover or regroup. Go in for the kill and end the encounter within the shortest possible time frame.

When you are legally and morally justified to use deadly force in your defense or the defense of another, there is no place for hesitation. When forced to fight for your life, be ready to pounce on the attacker at the first opportunity or sign of weakness. Turn into a human tornado, swarming him with an overwhelming attack until he no longer poses a threat.

When attacking, don't hesitate to use anything you can. In a real fight anything goes. Doing something unexpectedly can completely throw off the defender's game plan and give you a window of opportunity to gain the upper hand.

Pay attention to your opponent. Is he watching your blade too closely? Does he seem vulnerable to a punch or kick? Be deceptive and use your instincts.

Cut and kill can be as simple as a direct attack or as complex as a series of fakes, traps or angles. Here Ryan demonstrates a compound fluid trapping attack in cut and kill mode.

From saber, Ryan attacks suddenly getting the critical jump on the attacker and drawing first blood by cutting the closest target.

Ryan surges forward, following his assault with a trap from the defensive hand, securing the attacker's guard and paving the way his secondary attack.

Ryan controls the guard and delivers a swarm of over and under attacks to the throat and torso while moving to the outside of the attacker's centerline and away from his blade hand.

The arts of cut and run, cut and stay and cut and kill comprise the basic defensive strategies. But they are only concepts. In the real world, you will have to adapt to whatever your adversary and the situation throws at you and the ability to do so is at the heart of the next several chapters which focus on the strategy and tactics of the blade.

CHAPTER NINE

BLADE TACTICS

"If you want to learn to fight study technique.
If you want to learn to win, develop tactics."

– Richard Ryan

Tactical fighting is smart fighting. It is the application of techniques in direct relationship to a specific opponent and what he does or doesn't do. The superior fighter is constantly assessing both the situation and his adversary for weaknesses he may capitalize on. The master fighter chooses the very best technique to fit his immediate situation and applies it at the right moment. His actions are incidental, not accidental, as he stacks the deck in his favor against whatever threat he may face.

TACTICAL FIGHTING

Fighting tactically requires you to make quick assessments about an individual or a situation. Who is he? What level of skill might he possess? Is he strong or weak, fast or slow? Some things are easy to assess. For instance, is your opponent taller or shorter? This will translate into longer or shorter reach. Bigger or smaller is also easy as it often translates into levels of power and mobility. Other things such as a person's level of training are much harder to decipher, especially at the outset of a situation. Although things like stance, positioning and grip will give you some indication, they are by no means surefire. A good fighter will

adopt good positions. A better fighter will adopt the best positions. The problem, though, is that a great fighter just might bait you into a lethal trap by appearing to be pitifully ineffective or poorly skilled.

Miyamoto Musashi was arguably the most gifted Samurai warrior who ever lived. He is an enduring legend in Japan, where his exploits are celebrated in movies and books. Legend has it that he never lost a duel. Supposedly he became so skilled that he stopped using real swords later in life and killed many of his opponents with sticks, staffs and oars. In 1643, Musashi wrote *The Book of Five Rings*, a treatise on strategy based on the philosophy of five elements of life: fire, water, wind, earth and what he called the void. It was an accumulation of personal insights and strategies of war and well worth reading. To the uninitiated, much of the text can be confusing, but some things are decidedly simple and deadly.

In the chapter titled Fire, Musashi describes various methods of taking advantage of a situation. In one section he eludes to the idea of baiting his opponent into a death trap. He wrote: "In single combat, you can win by relaxing your body and spirit and then catching on to the moment the enemy relaxes, attack strongly and swiftly. You can also infect the enemy with a bored, careless or weak spirit."

In other words, make a show of being slow and then attack swiftly. A master fighter might lull you into believing you have the advantage, making you unprepared for a lightning fast attack. The point is that you can't judge a book by its cover. But masters of strategy are even more rare than good knife fighters. The likelihood that you run into one of them, let alone fight him, is astronomical. Still, if you want to win it is important to be aware of all the ways you might lose. In a conflict, you can make some educated guesses about your adversary that can give you an edge. Of course, once the conflict turns physical, you'll know about your opponent's abilities rather quickly.

Regardless, the smart fighter is always thinking. He's always updating his tactical information on his opponent and reevaluating what he might do to gain the advantage to finish the fight. Here are some questions you should think about for a single immediate opponent:

PRIMARY TACTICAL QUESTIONS:

ATTRIBUTES

1. Taller or shorter?
2. Bigger or smaller?
3. Athletic ability/probability?
4. Body language/aggression level/ attitude?

WEAPONS

1. What weapons does he/they have, if any?
2. Probability of concealing other weapons?
3. Specifics of weapons involved?

ENVIRONMENT

1. Other threats in close proximity?
2. Barriers and obstacles?
3. Are there other weapons in close proximity?

DURING THE ENCOUNTER

1. Offensive or defensive?
2. Stance and positional liabilities?
3. Initiation or recovery problems?
4. Repetitive/favored techniques?
5. Fast or slow?
6. Reactive abilities?
7. Response to actions?
8. Nervous or calm?

Now it would be ludicrous to think that you have time to consciously go down a checklist at the outset of a fight. You may not have time for anything except action. But going down a checklist is not the idea. The idea is to be aware of these tactical questions so that when an opponent presents an obvious answer to one of them, you recognize it and use it to your advantage. When answered, each one of these questions gives you a clue about what you may or may not do with your opponent. They help you prepare for what may come and provide valuable insights into tactics that can give you the winning edge. As an example, let's go through a quick rundown on an imaginary opponent using the questions outlined above.

QUICK PRE-CONFLICT ANALYSIS

Any pre-conflict analysis should start the moment you realize you are under threat of attack. The master fighter will sweep all thoughts from his mind except the situation at hand. He will flip a switch in his head, anticipating a sudden attack. At the same time he begins to take in tactical information, he may need to devise a survival strategy.

The first things you should assess are the most prominent physical attributes of the potential attacker. Bear in mind here, we are really only concerned about any obvious traits. If the person appears average in every respect, much of this would not apply and you deal with his actions accordingly. But if he presents an obvious attribute, say he's shorter and bigger than you are, you can use that observation against him. Let's say the aggressor is much bigger. He outweighs you by 60 to 80 pounds, most of which is not fat weight. He's also shorter than you and his body language and verbiage indicates he is cocky and aggressive. What does this mean to you tactically? It means that he is likely to be more powerful than you are. Weight, especially the lean muscle kind, means power. So you don't want to confront him directly. Shorter means that both in footwork and in reach you have a slight advantage, and aggressive means that he is likely to assume physical superiority over you and charge in at the first opportunity. Just knowing these few factors allows you to formulate a quick plan of attack. For example, a strategy might be to keep your distance, control the range as much as possible and place yourself in a position in which you can move freely. Perhaps you might put something between you, like a couch or fire hydrant to, hinder a sudden advance. From here a basic tactical plan might include quick strikes from a distance, attacking the closest target with the closest weapon to take advantage of your longer reach. If it is an unarmed conflict, you might launch a series of rapid fire jabs to the face or intersperse a quick kick or two to the lower legs to induce pain. If it is a knife fight, the tactics remain the essentially the same. Maneuver yourself into a position so you can move without obstruction and use your superior reach to cut his arms and body, retreating after each attack and whittling away at his resolve. Knowing he is aggressive, you should anticipate that at some point he will likely panic and try to corner you or

charge you. You should be ready for this, anticipating it by being ready to deliver a decisive counter when it happens. That is tactical fighting. Other questions that should be answered as quickly as possible include the possible or obvious use of other weapons on his part and a quick assessment of your immediate environment. Can you move freely or you restricted? Are there any other threats or weapons you may use in your defense? I am sure you get the picture.

One thing that must be said, however, is that even though you should always be analyzing your opponent, such analysis should never take the place of, nor interfere with, your ability to take immediate action. Analyzing an opponent for tactical weaknesses should become almost automatic and something that you do naturally before and during a fight. Don't get into paralysis by analysis. Remember that information doesn't win the war. It may help you to decide on a course of action, but it's the action that counts. Be smart and use your head, but be ready to unleash the animal inside you at a moment's notice.

KNIFE COMBAT

A knife fight, i.e., knife against knife, is only one of many possible self-defense scenarios you might find yourself in. Real fights, and more specifically the act of fighting in general, are sudden, brutal and often confusing. And weapons are not always the answer. You could be the greatest knife fighter in the world, but if an attacker jumps you by surprise, you'd better have plan B. Combat happens very quickly and sometimes without warning. Having been conditioned by movies and television to build up to violence with suspense and drama, most people are wholly unprepared for the suddenness of real combat. Think of it this way. How much time would it take for you to punch someone in the face from arms' distance? The average person can easily do it in 1/30th of a second, a quick individual can strike in less than 1/10th of a second, and a master can strike in half that. Now given these parameters, how many punches could a highly motivated person throw at you in five seconds? Even the slower person could rain a minimum of 15 punches on you in that time. A knife requires even less energy and range of motion than a punch, so put a knife in this person's hand and it could be 20 or more in the same time period.

When people are motivated, they can launch an assault with frightening speed. Look away for a moment, blink or drop your guard and "blam" the fight could be over before you know it. This is why it is so important to be aware and control the distance at all times. The sharpest knife and the greatest skill may not save you if you don't. On the other hand, if you have some training and control the range, you have a good chance of surviving even the swiftest attack. If you practice situational awareness, you might have the time to access your weaponry and dramatically change the odds.

KNIFE AGAINST KNIFE

All violent encounters are dangerous because people are dangerous. Whenever you face another human being bent on causing you harm, there is a good chance you will be hurt, injured or killed no matter what

you know. Training and knowledge provide countertactics, but are no guarantees that you will survive. The reason is that there are so many possible scenarios, situations, options, responses and methods of attack. However, of all the situations you may ever face, a fight with edged weapons is one of the absolute worst. Second to the firearm, the blade is the great equalizer. So if you ever find yourself in this unlucky situation, here are some tactics to remember:

1. Never fight fair. Fight to win at all cost. Fighting is not a dress rehearsal. When the real thing comes, you've got to be prepared to do anything and everything to win. Remember that the end result is the most important factor in a conflict. Do whatever you must to survive. This is the number one rule. Just because you're in a knife fight doesn't mean you can't punch, kick, grab, bite, throw something in the guy's face or grab another weapon. Cheat. There is no such thing as a fair knife fight. Reach down and grab a fistful of dirt or sand and throw it into the attacker's face and follow it with a decisive strike. You can throw anything for that matter. Dirt, rocks, detergent, a drink, anything to disrupt his attack. Throw a book, a phone, a glass, a shirt, coat or jacket. Grab a chair and toss it at him or use it as a shield. There are a thousand things you could do to confuse a would be attacker. Start thinking this way. This rule applies to all encounters, all weapons and all situations. When you're forced to use violence to stop violence, do whatever you must without hesitation.

2. Keep your distance. Use evasion as your primary means of defense. In a battle of weapons, counterattack is often the preferred tactic. Unless you're sure you can attack and overwhelm an attacker without effective retaliation on his part, don't attack. Make him run, lunge or reach

for you and cut him on the way in or out. In this way the attacker has two choices: try to catch you or quit. Often a determined foe will overcommit himself or his balance and be vulnerable to counter. In any case, no tactics will work unless you can consistently control the distance between you and your attacker.

3. Cut anything you can. Cut the hands, arms, legs, feet, face, body, anything you can reach, and especially the hand with the knife in it. You can often "de-fang the snake" this way. But any target is fair game. Lash out with your blade in a split second and return to your guard. Just keep cutting. You never know which cut will be the decisive one. In a life and death struggle, killer instinct is a must. The moment your assailant stops, hesitates or reacts to the pain or damage of one of your attacks or counters, pounce on him. Don't let him recover to start the dance all over again. When the moment of vulnerability comes, don't hesitate. Swarm your attacker with a series of fast, powerful slashes, stabs, punches and kicks until it's over.

4. Never assume immediate effect. You never know exactly how a cut from a knife will affect you or your opponent. A vicious looking cut that spews blood may, from a physiological standpoint, be superficial. On the other hand, a hairline slit in the body may be indicative of a fatal stab wound to a vital target. Regardless, always assume that nothing you do, no matter how decisive, will have an immediate effect on your attacker. Keep fighting until the end. People who have been fatally shot and stabbed have fought on long after they were technically dead and, in many instances, killed their attackers before checking out themselves. Always be ready to do more. The fights not over until it's over.

5. Be ready to change tactics. Since you never know what your opponent might do or when or how your attacks or counters will be effective, you need to be ready to change your strategy at any time. Don't beat a dead horse or you may be dead yourself. If something is not working, change your game plan. Switch tactics or do something unconventional. Spit, yell or throw something, whatever it takes. Always be ready and willing to alter your tactics in order to win. Only a fool fights on with ineffective techniques. Be flexible.

POSITIONAL ATTACKS

Positional attacks are attacks made as a result of the weaknesses or openings presented by an opponent's position or stance. They should be the first thing you look for in a knife fight. For example, an amateur might stick his knife out toward your face in a threatening manner, giving you the opportunity to cut it in response. Or, your opponent may adopt an unstable position allowing you to drive him off balance. Most often, positional attacks take the form or responses to bad guards which expose limb or body to sudden attack. I am constantly amazed at how many students and instructors alike are completely oblivious to their positions of liability. They adopt positions that expose themselves and wonder why they get cut. If you leave a door open, someone will walk through. If you stick it out there someone will take it off for you. It's that simple.

The following drawings represent common stances from various knife fighting systems. Each stance is shown with vital targets marked as exposed. Compare them to my combat stance. You make the decision as to which is best.

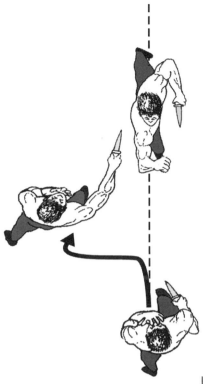

Positional attacks take advantage of weaknesses in centerline, stance and guard by exploiting mistakes and positions of liability. The most basic positional attack consists of attempting to get off centerline, thereby creating an angle of action that is difficult for the opponent to deal with.

In this example, you begin your attack parallel to centerline. As you engage, you quickly shift to the left of the attacker's body and angle in for a cut. The effect will be greatly enhanced by attempting to go to the opponent's blind side and away from the blade.

In combat, positional attacks can be very effective, so effective that they can often end a fight with a single move. Attacking with cunning and deception lengthens the opponent's reaction time and creates confusion, giving you the opportunity to decisively end the conflict.

Most knife fighting positions lack the necessary protection that is needed to survive a prolonged battle. Here we analyze the very popular military stance for weaknesses. Although it is a strong and stable position, the body is obviously open to direct attack. The guard hand is out in front and is often used like a windshield wiper to deflect incoming strikes. This requires perfect timing, because if you miss, your body is upright and open to assault.

A side view is even more telling. Notice how many obvious targets there are to attack and defend and the dramatic gap between the defensive hand and the body. In addition, by keeping the body upright on one vertical plane, the defender is forced to protect the entire upper and lower torso equally.

With just a cursory glance, you can see dramatic differences between an upright position and that of the Dynamic Combat crouch. In a knife fight, being smaller and more compact is definitely an advantage.

The only perfect position in a knife fight is behind a wall somewhere with a gun. When this isn't possible, the Dynamic Combat stance is far superior to other positions when it comes to improving your chances of survival. The DCM stance restricts direct access to vital body targets by compressing the body cavities and placing the skeletal muscular structure of the arm in front of the body's central line for protection.

This provides a wall of muscle and bone that protects the heart, lungs and abdomen. Instead of having numerous obvious targets, the stance eliminates direct assault to all areas except the eyes, and there is no way to protect them adequately without wearing a steel helmet. The face being the only obvious target, most attackers will focus their attacks to this single area which, in turn, makes your defensive decision simpler.

In addition, the "S" shape configuration of the body removes the lower abdomen from the same line of attack as the head. Notice that the abdomen is a full body width behind the head and throat. For an attacker to reach it, he must commit himself deep into the area where the blade is positioned. A dangerous proposition, to say the least.

KNIFE VERSUS
THE UNARMED ASSAILANT

Legally and morally there are few situations in which you can use a knife against someone who is unarmed. Being a deadly weapon, you must be in imminent fear of severe bodily harm or death when you choose to deploy a knife in self-defense. When an attacker has the ability and means to harm you and is wielding a weapon himself, you can usually use whatever means are necessary to survive, including fighting back with a weapon of your own. However, if the attacker is unarmed or the situation is sketchy and you can deal with the threat using a lower level of force, do so. It's the right thing to do, and you just might save yourself from a legal nightmare.

On the other hand, if there is a large discrepancy of force, i.e., the attacker is much bigger or stronger than you, or there is more than one of them, the edged weapon is a viable and often justified option. Always remember that you will be judged by the actions you take. Do what you must to survive the situation and no more. Escape at the first opportunity, no matter how much you are in control or how much you may want to stay and teach your attacker(s) a lesson.

If you choose to use an edged weapon against an unarmed attacker or a lesser threat, it is wise to avoid potentially lethal attacks. This can be done relatively easily by targeting the large muscle groups of the body and avoiding potentially deadly targets. It's really difficult for an attacker to chase you if you just buried your blade to the hilt in his thigh. It's even harder to grab or punch you if you've slashed his forearm or stabbed his biceps four or five times. If someone bigger and stronger than you grabs you, and you have access to your knife, cut the hand that

holds you. If necessary, perform multiple stabs, dice or fillet cuts to the connecting limb. Pry the attacker off or hit him and run. These attacks are not likely to be lethal but they will be effective.

Here John conceals the blade in a cross hand carry stance, positions himself outside the kill zone and negotiates with Lance as a potential attacker.

Lance suddenly lunges and is intercepted with a stab right through the hand. If you are both legally and morally justified to use an edged weapon in self-defense against an unarmed attacker, you have a tremendous advantage. No one in his right mind would knowingly enter a boxing match with an opponent who had a razor-sharp spike on the end of one glove.

A great equalizer, the edged weapon can be used to escape a grappling attack by someone of greater size and strength. Here John counters a strangle hold with a stab to the leg. By aiming your counterattacks at the large muscle groups of the attacker's limbs, you diminish the chances of killing him accidentally, while providing an incentive for the attacker to let you go.

KNIFE AGAINST THE IMPACT WEAPON

An impact weapon is a momentum-driven tool. It requires velocity to work. You've got to throw it or swing it, pick up momentum and make contact with a breakable area of the body. This is its greatest advantage and its greatest drawback. Don't get me wrong. An impact weapon can be lethal in the hands of someone who knows how to use it mechanically and tactically. One of my next books will be devoted entirely to the science of impact tools. However, on a technical level, the edged weapon has many more advantages than an impact tool, the foremost being that it is a touch weapon that requires very little force and velocity. Unlike the razor or knife, you can't just touch someone with a stick or rub it on his skin and be effective. But that doesn't necessarily mean someone armed with a knife will win a fight against someone armed with a stick. Any weapon can defeat any weapon. The key ingredients to combat effectiveness are knowledge, technical skill, tactical deployment, timing and luck, not necessarily the weapons involved.

To defeat an impact tool, the first rule is don't let the attacker get any free shots in, especially to vulnerable targets. Protect the head at all costs and try to time your attack to catch the assailant before or after a swing. Avoid running into the area of maximum force at the apex of his swing. If you're close enough when he starts to swing, surge forward and trap the weapon arm before he can pick up any real force. Stay right on top of him and impale him with the blade. If he's got the advantage of distance on you, stay away from him until you can time an assault. Let him swing at the air until you can explode into the kill zone, trap and counter. Either way, the strategy is simple. Stay way out or stay way in. The middle ground will get you clobbered.

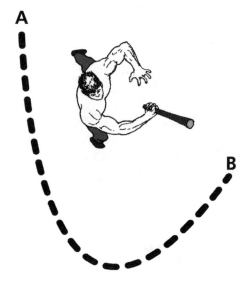

A

B

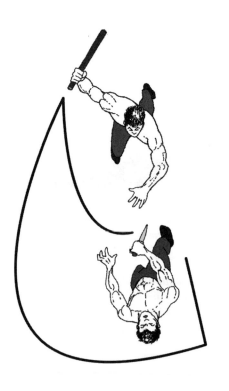

No single weapon is automatically superior to all others. The man
behind the weapon and his method of deployment are far more important.
For example, a quick accurate strike with an impact weapon to the knife
hand can disarm the blade, ending any advantage rather quickly.

...and if you're not careful, it could end your life. In combat, victory is a matter of techniques, tactics and the seizing of opportunity. Make the situation work for you, not against you.

The most important thing to remember about dealing with an impact weapon is to try to avoid intersecting the attacker's line of force. Stay well away from him, or get inside right on top of him and you nullify his effectiveness. Don't try to fight him in his home run zone.

When the attacker swings, evade or block his attack and move to the inside of his arc of force while protecting your bio-computer. Neutralize his attack and trap his weapon as you counter. Stay right with him, driving him back so he cannot swing again.

KNIFE AGAINST THE GUN

The legendary Japanese swordsman Miyamoto Musashi lived during the time of the inventions of gunpowder and the firearm, about which he wrote: "At a distance, firearms have no equal, but when swords are crossed, firearms are useless." Of course, he based this observation on the firearms of ancient Japan. One wonders what his specific observation would be if the ancient Japanese warrior had included an MP-5 submachine gun as part of his arsenal? In any case, I'm sure the spirit of the observation would remain the same. What Musashi meant was that in close, where most real combat occurs, a man armed with a firearm has a distinct disadvantage against a man with a edged weapon, especially the long sharp kind. Think about it. For the sake of argument, let's say you've got a handgun, and I've got a samurai sword. We are at conversational distance. Assuming you have your gun out, you must still point, fire and kill me instantly before I can sever your limbs or cleave your body in two. Not likely to happen. If you have the weapon in a holster, you can forget it all together. Better make

your peace because you'll never even clear leather before your blood hits the pavement.

Granted, the sword has the advantages of length, leverage and cutting surface over the tactical folder or fixed blade knife, but the idea is the same. A highly skilled knife fighter will kill the trained firearm's aficionado at close range nine out of ten times and the reverse is true at a distance or if obstacles are involved. But it must be said that part of the reason someone armed with an edged weapon is so dangerous is that people trained with firearms are rarely skilled in hand-to-hand and nonballistic weapons combat. I have met countless firearms people, both novice and professional, who haven't the slightest clue of how to effectively throw or block a punch, stop a grappling attack, or defend against a club, or beer bottle, let alone a razor sharp blade. Many believe that the power of the firearm will solve all their problems. Remember when I said that if you don't acknowledge reality, it will automatically work against you. This is a prime example. Underestimate the blade and you may lose your life.

STOPPING THE BALLISTIC WEAPON

Access, distance and controlling the line of fire are the three most important factors when engaging someone with a firearm. The first factor, access, will determine your overall actions and those of your opponent. For example, if your attacker has his weapon drawn and pointed at your head and your knife is safely tucked away in your pocket - forget the knife! You have a much better chance deflecting or trapping the firearm and punching him in

the head repeatedly than trying to go for your blade. Conversely, if the attacker has his weapon in a holster, his pants, or better yet, in a fanny pack and you have your knife in your hand, use the knife! It all depends on who has access to what at any given time. This is another reason why you want to be well rounded. To be effective, martial artists should explore conventional weaponry and firearms people should learn hand-to-hand combat skills.

closer is better. I would much rather my assailant shove his gun in my face than cautiously control me from a distance. If possible, use deception and negotiate the range before you take action. Pretend to surrender or feign a heart attack; anything to throw him off and cover a few feet of distance. But be warned the advantage of a firearm is it's simplicity. A person need only point and pull the trigger and you could be dead. So be ready to fight or flee in an instant.

DISTANCE

Remember that distance controls time. When dealing with a firearm, the control of the time/distance variable it critical. How fast can you cover the ground between you and your opponent? Can he get a shot off in time, or can you kill him first? These are all factors of distance and access, and are unique to every situation. You may be standing a few yards from your opponent, but there is a couch between you. How will that affect your ability to get to him effectively? As a general rule when dealing with a firearm,

LINE OF FIRE

A bullet is a very small piece of metal, but it is a piece of metal that can travel at speeds exceeding a mile a second. Everyone realizes its combative advantage. However, to be effective, the trajectory of this small piece must hit you. The line of fire is the exact path the bullet travels after the trigger is pulled. If this path intersects with a vital area of your body when the gun is fired, the game is over. But this is harder to do than most people think. The line of fire is a thin one. Unless you're shot at with a bazooka, the line of fire is only a few millimeters in diameter. A gun pointed at your head need only be deflected a few inches to allow for your survival. In a conflict with a firearm, be aware of exactly where the line of fire is at any given time and especially when you attack. When you take action, move out of the line of fire or deflect it and stick with the attacker like glue, cutting, slashing and neutralizing his attempts to use his weapon. Deflect it, trap it, grab it, hit it, whatever works, but stay right on top of him until you have disarmed him and ended the threat.

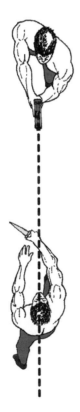

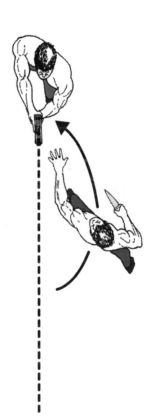

Just because you are carrying a weapon doesn't mean you should use it. The edged weapon may be a devastating defensive tool, but it's still a tool. Unless you plan to carry it open and ready all the time, you may have trouble getting to it when you need it. If you can't access it immediately in a time of need, you need to resort to plan "B."

Here, both men have weapons. Lance has a handgun in a holster where he can get to it very quickly. John has a tactical folder which, at this range, can be the superior weapon. However, his folder is tucked away in his pocket where he can't get to it.

Knowing this, he ignores his knife and traps Lance as he reaches for the firearm. He drives into him, controlling the weapon and delivering multiple strikes to the head and throat.

With the blade out, it's a different story. Here, at a distance of 10 feet, John has the advantage because Lance still has to draw, aim, fire and hit either the brain or the brainstem to stop John in his tracks. That is incredibly difficult to do in a fraction of a second and against a moving target.

As Lance reaches for his weapon, John bolts forward, cutting the gun hand.

John continues his attack, driving into Lance, trapping and deflecting the firearm out of the line of fire and cutting his throat. You should always remember that someone can run forward faster than you can run backward.

MULTIPLE ATTACKERS

Fighting more than one person at a time qualifies as an extreme life-threatening situation. Even if the attackers have no weapons and they are physically inferior, their combined mass, weight and possible angles of attack make this situation extremely dangerous, especially in confined spaces. Throw a weapon or two into the mix and you have the makings of a nightmare.

If you are threatened or attacked by multiple assailants, the same rules apply that apply to a one-on-one confrontation - escape! If you can't and are in imminent danger, attack them, hitting the closest or the weakest one first with everything you've got. If you go at them with sudden fury, they may flee, or at

least hesitate, giving you a window of opportunity to take a few of them out and make tracks. If you cannot flee yourself, try to escalate. Get a weapon. Any weapon. A knife, stick or gun is preferred but a pen, pencil, ash tray, glass, beer bottle, broom handle, phone, lamp, rock or chair will do. Don't fight fair in a situation that is obviously unfair. Grab anything you can to give you an edge, no pun intended.

When applying weapons to a multiple opponent situation, the first thing you must realize is that you can't afford event the slightest mistake. Armed or unarmed multiple attackers can overrun you, confusing your defenses with multiple angles and lines of attack. Miss a single strike or blow and the fight could be over as they

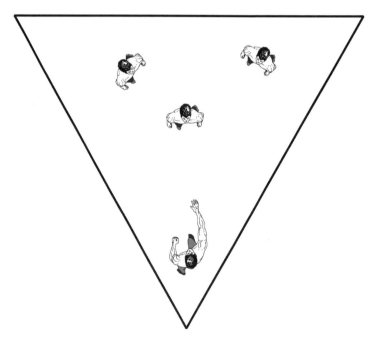

One of the greatest advantages that multiple assailants have over you is the ability to overwhelm your position and your senses with a variety of attacks and angles of engagement. When threatened with such a situation, the first thing you should try to do is maneuver so that they are all in your direct line of sight.

swarm you to the finish. Against unarmed attackers, it's bad enough, but against armed multiple attackers you have to be immediately effective and get the hell out of there.

The good news is that there is a phenomenon that occurs in multiple opponent situations. I call it time distortion. It is the disruption of our sense of time, space and distance when we are thrust into situations with extreme sensory overload. With multiple attackers moving at different rates of speed, from different angles, time distortion is the inability of our senses to judge what is occurring correctly. If you remain passive, time distortion can work against you as you try to stop every single action without retaliation or movement. In other words, if you just stand there and try to defend you'll lose. You'll lose not only because you are facing multiple opponents, but because your senses cannot keep up with the onslaught. However, the good news is that time distortion can work for you and it can work easily and dramatically.

I have fought multiple opponents on quite a few occasions. I guess this is because most criminals and street toughs travel in packs both for safety and to enhance their meager courage. I have had the unfortunate experience of being attacked before by two, three and even four people. I have even been the unwilling participate in a few knock down drag out fights you would have to call mini riots.

I have never lost a fight. But the closest I ever came was the first time I was involved in a multiple assailant situation. Had the situation been slightly different, it would probably have been the first time. I was lucky because there were only two of them and I had warning. I saw it coming, but I didn't act quick enough. I took them both out, but it took much longer than it should have. It

was sudden and confusing. I had experienced time distortion for the first time and wasn't sure what was going on. I began to vigorously experiment with the phenomenon, sparring two or more opponents every opportunity I had. I began to learn.

Dealing with multiple assailants is dramatically different than dealing with one person. In some respects it is much harder dealing with one, completely ready, skilled individual. When two skilled fighters square off with one another, there is little perceptual distortion or confusion. They face and watch

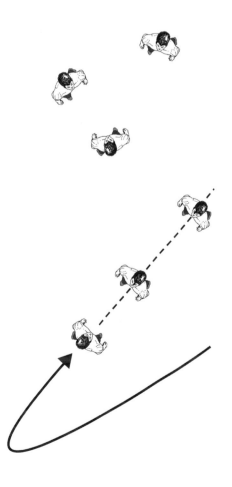

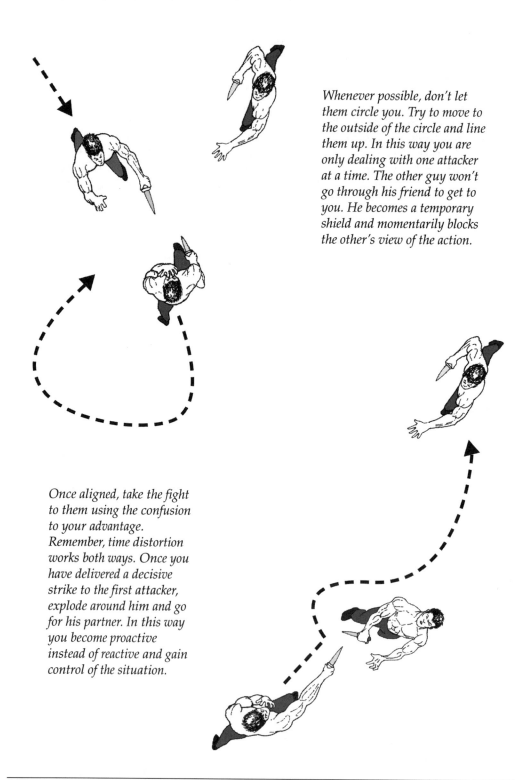

Whenever possible, don't let them circle you. Try to move to the outside of the circle and line them up. In this way you are only dealing with one attacker at a time. The other guy won't go through his friend to get to you. He becomes a temporary shield and momentarily blocks the other's view of the action.

Once aligned, take the fight to them using the confusion to your advantage. Remember, time distortion works both ways. Once you have delivered a decisive strike to the first attacker, explode around him and go for his partner. In this way you become proactive instead of reactive and gain control of the situation.

If they have you surrounded and won't let you get to the outside, or there are barriers that hinder your mobility, switch tactics. Instead of lining them up, spread them apart. Doing so prohibits them from getting organized and taking unified action. Become a human tornado, spinning from one attacker to the next, and back again, until they are both down or you find a way to escape the battle.

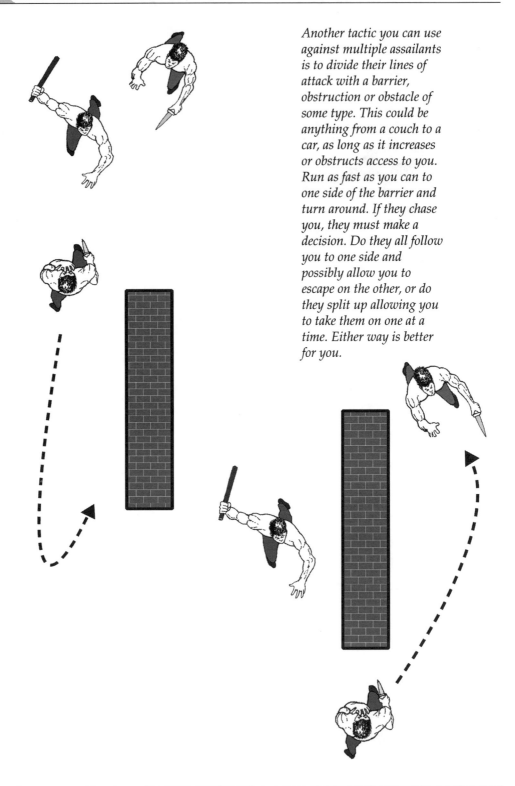

Another tactic you can use against multiple assailants is to divide their lines of attack with a barrier, obstruction or obstacle of some type. This could be anything from a couch to a car, as long as it increases or obstructs access to you. Run as fast as you can to one side of the barrier and turn around. If they chase you, they must make a decision. Do they all follow you to one side and possibly allow you to escape on the other, or do they split up allowing you to take them on one at a time. Either way is better for you.

each other with ruthless concentration and focus. Like two tigers circling for the kill, they are never more ready to fight. Throw a third person into the fray, and all hell breaks loose. Now that extreme concentration is divided among multiple combatants. Confusion makes for poor perception. But if you're smart, you can make this confusion work for you by becoming proactive and taking the fight to them.

If all of you are unarmed, try to line them up so you only have to deal with them one at a time. If they are circling you and that's not possible, spread them apart by alternating your attacks between them. Hit hard and fast, with linear power blows aimed at the head or throat. It is important that you not spend more than a split second with each individual before attacking his companions. If you get locked onto one person, his buddies may clock you. Move from attacker to attacker swiftly. When you see an opening where you can escape, take it.

If you are armed with a knife and they have no weapons, use good judgment. If you have the luxury of space and distance and can move, you may want to use less than lethal attacks such as slashes to their arms, legs and face. If you are trapped or are sure they will likely kill you if they get a hold of you, intersperse linear stabs to the body, face and throat with your slashing attacks.

If the attackers are armed, it becomes much more complex. What do they have? Guns? Knives? Bottles? A mixture of weapons? How far away are they? Who is the most accessible? Do I need to go after the guy with the gun first, or can I shield against him with his buddy?

Multiple assailants with weapons is complex art unto itself. I expect to write an entire book on this in the future. Regardless, it's important to keep it simple and use your instincts. If you can get the jump on them with the element of surprise, do it! For example, you might give in and pretend like you're going to hand your knife over to one of them. When you get close, flip the blade in your hand and cut him on your way to his partner. In these situations common sense and instinct go a long way. Use the same principles you would against unarmed attackers but add trapping, blocks or deflections to the mix to control the opponents' weapons. Take the fight to them. Make them worry about their own safety and escape at the first opportunity.

Whether you face a gun, knife, club or fists, the main factor is the ability to use whatever you have available. Use deception and cunning to throw them off their game and employ the element of surprise to your advantage. When you cross the line into action, explode on your opponents, never letting them get a chance to recover or retaliate. Once you have the advantage, press it. Stay right on top of them and finish them off. This concept of "attack the attacker" applies to almost any self-defense situation, especially this one. Make the attacker worry about his own safety, not how he is going to get through your defenses and get to you. Use defense only when you have no other option or when you find yourself squared up with a really dangerous person that requires you to outthink and outmaneuver him to survive. Be aggressive. Be smart and stay alive.

CHAPTER TEN

BLADE STRATEGIES

" Combat is a physical game of chess."

– Richard Ryan

A strategy is a overall game plan, while a tactic includes the individual techniques and maneuvers necessary to achieve that plan. Strategies and tactics deploy specific techniques and maneuvers that are designed to meet and defeat an adversary under advantageous conditions. Tactical and strategic fighting is smart fighting. They represent the art of using your opponent's weaknesses against himself while positioning yourself to deploy your strengths. It is power and skill directed by intelligent thought.

THE FIVE TYPES OF FIGHTERS

Dynamic Combat defines five types of fighters. In general terms, the five types of fighters represent the five ways a person will fight in battle. Everyone falls into one of these categories because the types are based on the human nature we all possess. When placed under stress, certain aggressive patterns emerge and dominate our performances. The greater the stress, the more these pattern characteristics will manifest themselves. The five types are chargers, blockers, runners, sluggers and the very rare fifth type, we'll call the synergists.

The first type, the charger, is considered the most dangerous type of fighter, at least at the outset of a fight. The charger will explode at you suddenly, trying to overwhelm you with force and sheer ferocity. This type of fighter has learned the value of speed and aggression. He can be the most dangerous because of the ferocity of his assault.

The blocker is perhaps the most common type of fighter, because blocking is instinctive for most people. Unlike the charger, the blocker stands his ground with a strong defense stopping and countering your attacks. He will often wait for you to make the first move, drawing you out and then launching his own counter assault.

The runner is a hit and run artist. He hits and moves, moves and hits. He is very defensive, but don't underestimate him. He can be Mohammed Ali at his zenith. Deceptive, elusive and evasive, he never seems to be where you thought he was a moment ago. The runner will use footwork to evade contact with you and get you to overcommit. Then he'll often change gears, stand his ground and knock you out when you least expect it.

But it is the slugger who is the knockout artist. Usually tough, rugged and powerful, the slugger is often willing to take a blow to give one. Sometimes forgoing defense altogether, this juggernaut will march forward throwing bombs until he lands one and takes you out.

Ninety-nine percent of all people on the planet are by nature one of these first four types. At first glance, some people may seem otherwise, but when push comes to shove they will reveal their true natures. What martial arts they have studied (or not studied) has very little to do with it. For example, let's say that you have a big strong guy who spent most of his life playing football. He is a powerhouse, genetically and psychologically gifted toward the use of power and force. But he is fascinated with the style and grace of Chinese martial arts and takes up the study of Wing Chun Kung Fu. Wing Chun is a 400 year old Chinese martial art that is supposed to have been created by the Buddhist nun Nu Moi. Legend has it she couldn't compete with the strength and power of men, so she designed a system around the use of finesse and precision to defeat her opponents. Wing Chun teaches considerable motor skills, constant physical control and economical action. Wing Chun is a simple and great martial art. It was the only art the late great Bruce Lee ever formally studied. What does this have to do with types of fighters you may ask. Well, getting back to our football playing friend, let's say

he studies Wing Chun for three years. That's about how long it takes to learn the entire system. He's good at it. Then one day he gets in a fight with a real dangerous person. He attempts to use his Wing Chun training but his attacker is elusive and ready for him. Blam, blam! He takes a couple of hits to the face and his blood flows. Suddenly all his stylized Wing Chun training goes out the window. Furious, his true nature comes out and he charges his opponent, throwing haymakers in every direction. Why does he do this? Because his true nature is a slugger and under stress it manifested. A person's true nature can be subdued and controlled by training, but never erased.

THE SYNERGIST

The fifth type of fighter is the most rare of all. The fifth type is the synergist, a fighter who becomes all of the other four types. His training supersedes his nature. Through extensive work, experience, mental discipline and self control he actually overrides his true nature. More accurately, he learns to control and focus, becoming whatever he needs to become in a given conflict. This is rare indeed and a focal point of the art of Dynamic Combat. This is the goal all students of DCM strive for.

The synergist is by far the most dangerous of them all. He is the chameleon who blends into any situation and adapts to any opponent. If you are a charger, he becomes the consummate runner. If you are a runner, he becomes the slugger. He adapts to his environment and situation. It takes years of training to even approach this level of expertise in real combat, which is perhaps why this type of fighter remains an ideal to most.

KNIFE FIGHTING STRATEGIES

When weapons are deployed, the five types of fighters remain essentially the same. Tools don't change the carpenter. The only things that do change when someone is armed are the specific attack and counter methods. For example, if a person is a charger by nature, he will still be a charger with weapon in hand, but his method of assault will be different. He will attempt to deploy the advantages of the weapon under the guise of a charger.

THE BLADE CHARGER

Chargers with edged weapons are swarmers. Because the edged weapon is a touch weapon, it has the advantage of coming at you from any conceivable angle. The blade charger will use this to "swarm" his opponent with a hurricane-like attack. He will try to get the critical jump on you because he knows that action is faster than reaction. He will explode at you suddenly, trying to run you over, cutting and slashing in a whirlwind of steel. Because of the ferocity of his attack, this type of fighter is the most dangerous of them all. If you are unprepared, the charger can take even a seasoned fighter by surprise. He wants to pounce on you when you least expect it and land a series of telling strikes, overwhelming the defense and ending the fight before it gets started.

Because of this, the first rule of defensive combat strategy (armed or unarmed) is to always assume that everyone you face is a charger until proven otherwise. Let me repeat that. Always assume everyone you face is going to explode forward and jump you the moment the fight starts. In this way you become mentally and physically prepared to respond instantly. If the fighter turns out to be another type, say a runner, that's great. Deal with him appropriately. If possible, get to open ground. Always keep your distance in anticipation of a sudden attack. The more distance, the better. Distance and space allow you to draw him

out. The more you can get him to chase you, the more momentum, he will pick up in his attacks. The more the momentum the harder it will be for him to change direction mid-motion. This will allow you to stop hit him and sidestep his attacks, cutting him as he goes by. But be ready to cut and stay at any moment should you find yourself in a confined space.

THE BLADE SLUGGER

The blade slugger is a madman with a blade. He is a hacker who comes at you with full force, trying to separate you from your limbs or drive his blade through the back of your spine. He commits to his attack 100 percent trying to end the conflict by sheer aggression and force. If you're unprepared, he will hack through your defenses and end your life before you know it.

Defeating a hacker is much like dealing with the charger. Keep your distance and draw him out. Make him overcommit his power and reach by retreating straight back and at a 45 degree angle instead of side stepping to the right or left. The blade slugger may not have the same momentum as the charger does, and if you sidestep you will still be in the kill zone. He will simply follow you hacking away. Stay away from him and pick your counterstrokes carefully. Attack his swinging limbs by inserting your blade into the arc of his swings as they pass. The hatchet grip would be a good idea so you don't lose your blade on contact. Let his power do the damage for you, then retreat and counter. When he loses his position or reacts to a cut in his limbs, go in for the kill.

THE BLADE BLOCKER

The blade blocker is usually a stylist with a blade and a technician that can be well versed in the mechanics of knife fighting. He could have studied Kali, Silat, or any number

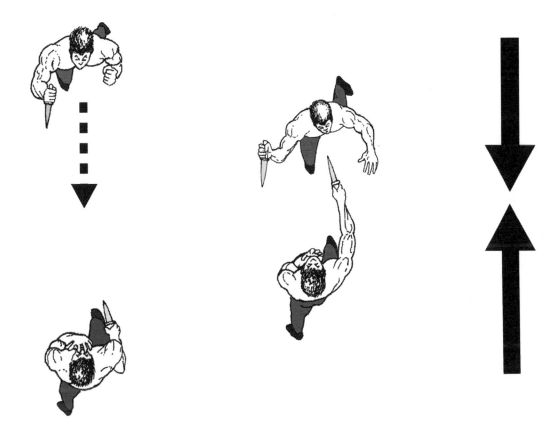

The charger is the most dangerous fighter because he can overwhelm you before you know what has happened. Often, his objective is to catch you by surprise and run you down with little or no warning. He is the element of surprise personifed. To avoid becoming his victim, it is smart to always assume that everyone you meet is a charger until he proves otherwise. In this way, you prepare yourself to deal with a sudden violent assault at the outset of every confrontation. If he fails to charge and is obviously another type of fighter, you adjust your strategy accordingly.

One of the most effective ways of dealing with a charger is to not let him charge you, but stop hit him with a preemptive strike. Think of it as old time gunfighting. Two guys meet in the street and square up to draw down on one another. They lock eyes and one slaps leather, but before his gun clears his holster, he's dead. The other guy was faster and ready for him, shooting him first. Remember, speed and postion are 90 percent of the game. Get as close to the opponent as possible and watch for telltale clues that he his going to launch an attack, like setting a drive leg or tensing to pounce. When he moves, intercept him with a direct strike and move off his line of attack.

Another strategy for dealing with the charger is to sidestep his advance. Doing so requires that he picks up as much momentum as possible and you time your evasion perfectly. If you try to do this from too close a range or when he has acquired little momentum, it will not work because he will be able to turn with you and continue his attack.

The idea is to draw him out and make him chase you. The more he chases you, the more momentum he will pick up. Remember Newton's third law of physics: "Objects in motion tend to stay in motion until acted on by an external force." The more momentum, the harder it is to change directions midstream.

To sidestep a charger, bait him by dropping your guard and exposing your vitals or by appearing that you are not ready to deal with an advance. Be sure not to let him too close if you do this. Remember, someone can run forward faster than you can run backwards, so give yourself some reaction distance. When he attacks, wait until the last possible instant and step to the side, slashing or stabbing him as he goes by.

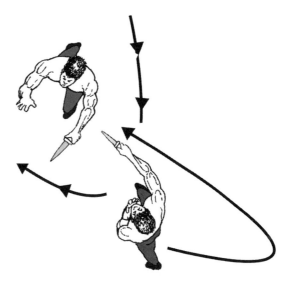

The slugger/hacker is like facing the grim reaper. He slashes and stabs at you so violently that it can be terrifying. His objective is to catch you with one or two devastating strikes that end the fight, and perhaps your life, in a decisive manner. Because of his reckless abandon for his own safety, dealing with him can be very difficult and is hard to do safely.

The good news is that most skilled individuals are not blade sluggers. Skilled fighters know it is profoundly foolish to commit everything you have with each attack. Therefore, most hackers you face will be amateurs who will telegraph and over commit their actions, making them extremely vulnerable to surgical attacks. The slugger will usually set himself before he launches into a volley. Like the charger, he can be effectively stop hit, intercepting his initial actions before they become too powerful. Another effective strategy is to bait him into overcommitting and then counter before he can recover. To do this, extend the response line out of his immediate range. Tempt him by dropping your guard slightly or otherwise putting yourself into a position of false vulnerability. When he attacks, snap back out of range and reengage him with a strike before he can recover his balance and position.

of other arts, or he could have simply read a few books and bought a few videos on the subject. He could be a master or an novice, but he has some concept of technique and application. His movement can be deceptive and confusing, often on purpose.

Because the blocker stylist could be versed in a wide variety of styles and methods, there is no way of giving you an exact strategy against him. You have to take it on a case-by-case basis. But I can tell you one thing. Many styles of knife fighting are complex, using fine motor skills that are difficult to perform under stress. Often, complex or fancy moves are used to confuse and intimidate. Many oriental styles of combat deploy such deceptive tactics. I found out early on that if you plant a fast, direct attack right in the middle of someone's fancy techniques, they will usually go down wondering what hit them. Fight complexity with simplicity. When he's whipping his blade around and assuming some scary looking postures, keep it simple. Strike fast. Strike anything you can reach and repeat it as needed. If he begins to pick up on what you're doing (assuming you give him the time to do so), change tactics. Intersperse your direct attacks with indirect ones. Mix in some simple fakes so he will never know which one is the real attack. Be quick. Be unpredictable and you can handle the most deceptive and confusing type of fighter.

THE BLADE RUNNER

The blade runner is the hit and run artist. He is a fencer with a knife. His objective is to keep his distance and slash and stab anything he can reach until he can deliver a decisive strike. He is the essence of our cut and run strategy. If skilled and quick on his feet, he can be frustrating and deadly.

The blade runner is hard to beat because he is hard to reach. He seldom overcommits and will take advantage of you if you do so. Like smoke, he seems to be one place and when you strike at him, "poof," he's somewhere else. Leave an opening, however slight, and he will penetrate it and disappear before you can retaliate. The trick to defeating him is not to fence with him. Don't allow him the luxury of his strategy. Threaten him with short, direct attacks and fakes on his guard and drive him into a corner or corner him with an object, such as a car or a table. Take away his ability to retreat and he must change his game plan entirely. Another strategy is to intersperse sudden alternative striking attacks. Switching from saber to ice pick or hatchet grip allows you to hit with a solid fist. The knife acts like a Kobuton or a role of quarters, stabilizing the hand and making for a mallet-like blow. With the focus on the knife, this is often completely unexpected. You can suddenly explode with either hand landing a punch to the face or throat when he least expects it. You can whip a kick to his inner knee joint or thigh and send him to the ground where it's much harder to hit and run. One warning though. If you use any alternative tactics, you'd better make them really quick and deceptive. Get his attention on the blade first and then drop another attack on him. Never do this on a completely ready knife fighter and never do this from long range. Get in as close as possible and use deception. From a defensive standpoint, it's good to remember that these things could also happen to you when you deploy the cut and run strategy.

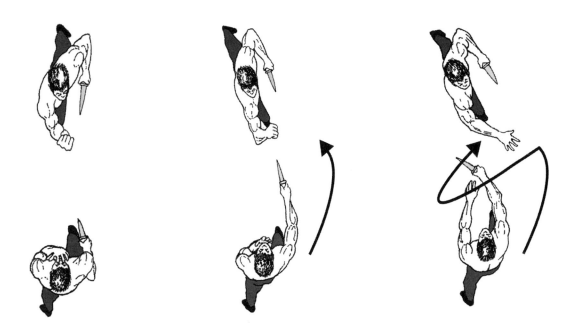

The blocker is usually not a very mobile fighter. He likes to stand his ground and mix it up. His objective is to deal with your attack and launch a decisive counterattack of his own. People who stand toe-to-toe and block in a knife fight are either highly skilled or completely unskilled. The act of blocking is a natural protective response to a threat and everyone will do it when attacked suddenly. However, in a battle of blades, your blocks and parries must be perfect every time or you could be killed. Not good odds. If someone stands right on your doorstep and tries to block and counter, you should assume that he is a very skilled and dangerous person. If this proves to be untrue, that's great, but don't count on it.

Defeating a good blocker requires timing and cunning. He will likely be prepared for simple direct attacks, and may have a deadly counter waiting for you, so if you use direct attacks, make them really fast and simple. Attack his blocking limb or whatever you can reach without overcommitment. If you are very fast, speed may be all you need. He may not be able to keep up with your assault. However, if he can keep up and direct attacks are not working, change your strategy. Use indirect attacks. Extend your response line slightly to give yourself a safety zone and launch a vicious attack at a specific angle. When he goes to block it, switch you line of attack to another line or flow into a cut on the blocking limb. Mix up direct and indirect attacks until he becomes so confused that his blocking strategy falls apart.

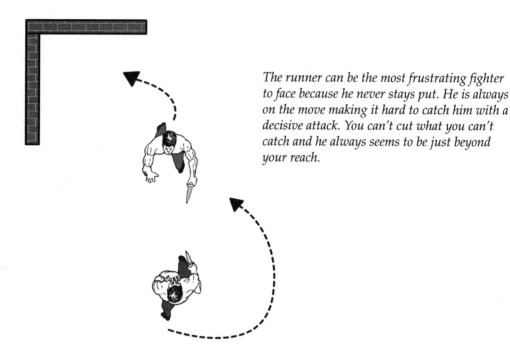

The runner can be the most frustrating fighter to face because he never stays put. He is always on the move making it hard to catch him with a decisive attack. You can't cut what you can't catch and he always seems to be just beyond your reach.

However, if you're fast you should be able to catch him, especially if you use your head. One of the best strategies against a runner is to do a quick assessment of your environment, locating any barriers or obstructions you might be able to use to corner him. When you find one, reorient the conflict so that his back is to the barrier. Once you do this, cut off the arena of battle by methodically chasing him with a sharp aggressive attack. As he nears the obstruction, he will begin to panic and try to escape. Don't let him. Keep moving laterally in a zig zag fashion cutting the range until he can no longer escape.

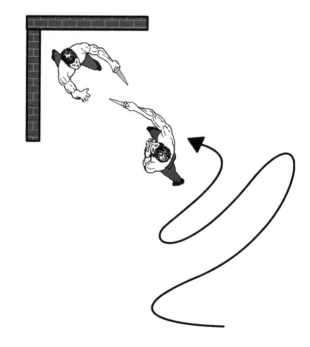

CHAPTER ELEVEN

DEADLY MISTAKES

"I'm not afraid to die. I just don't want to be there when it happens."

– Woody Allen

In any battle, you can lose in a variety of ways. But in a close quarter war of blades, you can lose even quicker. Like a gunshot, a slash of a blade could be fatal in a single act. Because of this, you must think, move and act in such a way as to not leave anything to chance. You must stack the deck in your favor with technical proficiency. Here are the deadly mistakes which dominate the landscape of combat.

LOSING POSITION

In its finest manifestation, the art of war is the art of positioning, much like a physical game of chess fighters maneuvering themselves into positions of advantage or finding themselves fighting for their lives in positions of liability. If it is you that finds yourself out of position and your attacker has an edged weapon, the game could be fatal. Always strive to retain a constant state of readiness. Stay coiled and ready to pounce like a cat, claws coiled in anticipation. But remember that no one is perfect and real fighting is not choreographed as in the movies and, to a large extent, your average martial arts school. If you find yourself off balance or off centerline, recover immediately and get back in the fight. Things happen. The experienced fighter knows this and is ready to adapt to whatever may occur. Stay balanced, track centerline and stay in the fight.

Another deadly mistake related to loss of position is lazy footwork. Not moving when you need to is the best way to force an unnecessary exchange of blades. Since footwork is the most important aspect of defense, the lack of it will put you in peril. If you find it hard to move, adjust your stance. Find a position that allows you to move with ease. Stay light on your feet and move, move, move!

OVERCOMMITMENT

Overcommitment is the act of overextending one's actions beyond the point of control. Whether we're talking about defense, offense or counter attack, overcommitting can be one of the most deadly mistakes you can make. Overcommitment of technique or action dramatically increases your recovery time and thus the time you are exposed to your opponent's counter attack. The longer your exposure, the greater the danger. Stay sharp and move with catlike economy. From the outset of a fight, endeavor to stay compact and economical. Keep your actions tight, thus keeping your exposure to a minimum. If you overextend an action, recover and regroup immediately. Strike like a coiled snake, snapping back into position with machinelike precision constantly ready to continue the fight.

MENTAL LAPSES

The mind controls the body; the body controls the tools. Without the mind, the body is useless. In combat, things can happen in the blink of an eye (or the flash of a blade) and you must stay mentally vigilant until the encounter is completely over. Never take your eyes off your attacker. You can't afford to lose perception or concentration even for a brief moment. By doing so, you could be caught in the shadow of Mr. Murphy and taken out. Keep ruthlessly calm. Focus your mind on the defeat of your attacker and don't allow anything to get in the way of this concentration. Stay in the fight till the bitter end, regardless of what happens.

HESITATION

The late Ed Parker, founder of Kenpo Karate was quoted as saying, "He who hesitates meditates in the horizontal position." What he meant was that if you hesitate, you'll be laid out. You must be prepared to take the advantage when it comes because it may not come again. Along with mental vigilance comes the determination to act whenever the opportunity presents itself. You must be

ready to strike at any moment because the moment may not come again. Master knife fighters are fast on their feet and almost never lose the position of advantage. They have unnerving concentration and never hesitate to act when the time comes. Adopt these qualities and you won't be caught off guard.

UNDERESTIMATION

Perhaps the greatest mistake a person can make is to underestimate an opponent. Human nature is unpredictable. You never know what someone is capable of or how they will act or react. The guy who looks jolly, drives a nice car, wears an expensive suit and speaks softly may be a ruthless scumbag drug dealer. That 13 year old skinny kid may be an amoral gang banger who will kill you just as look at you. When it comes to violence, there's no such thing as an average person. When spurned to violence, people can become unbelievably savage and ruthless. That articulate, seemingly civilized person may only loosely hide an uncontrollable violent temper. Male or female, young or old, strong or weak; it makes no difference. Everyone can become unimaginably brutal under the right circumstances. Always assume anyone you find yourself in a conflict with is extremely dangerous.

When thrust into a problem situation, it's time to press your paranoia buttons. On the outside you should stay calm and relaxed. Internally, you should be preparing for the worst. Erase the external image of your aggressor from your mind and focus on what he is saying and doing. Remember, it's only actions that count. Don't let a person's age, gender, appearance, physical condition or demeanor fool you. If possible, be civil and try to de-escalate the situation, but be prepared for instant retaliation should it become necessary. Whenever I have found myself in a potentially violent situation, I flip a switch in my head and jump to an extreme state of mind. The moment I recognize a threat directed at me, I immediately assume that this person could try to kill me right now. In this way my mind prepares itself for the most extreme scenario. I teach my students to work backwards from this point of view. When threatened, I look for a reason to not drop my attacker where he stands. Because I don't want to fight, I'm hoping he will give me a reason not to engage him. By adopting an extreme mindset, you won't be caught napping if the situation suddenly explodes beyond your expectations. Never underestimate the brutality of the human species.

CHAPTER TWELVE

THE DEADLY MIND

"Knowledge is the antidote for fear."

– Ralph Waldo Emerson

No work on real fighting would be complete unless it addresses the physiological aspects of interpersonal combat. You could be young, strong and powerful and have the greatest techniques known to man, but if you don't have it upstairs, you'll lose. Your mindset, your ability to deal with violence and extreme physical and mental stress, is perhaps the most important attribute you may possess. In a potentially lethal situation such mental toughness and determination is critical.

UNDERSTANDING FEAR

Fear is defined by Webster's as "an unpleasant often strong emotion caused by the anticipation or awareness of danger." That definition hardly does it justice. Fear is one of man's big three emotions. Along with love and hate, fear governs our lives to a great extent. We fear the IRS. We fear public speaking. We fear losing our jobs and we even carry with us some primal fears genetically bred into our psyche such as fear of the dark or spiders and reptiles. Edged weapons tap into our primal fears. They pull on our minds, taking us back to a time when man feared being torn limb from limb by his fellow creatures. If you doubt this, note your reaction when someone hands you a razor sharp combat fighting knife. How do you react? I know how I react – with great respect and just a little trepidation. It's natural to fear things that can harm us. Fear itself is natural. Without it man would have been extinct long ago. Fear is nature's early warning signal. It tells us that we could be in danger and revs us up to fight or flee.

When you feel great fear, your body goes into a mild state of shock. The blood which normally flows freely throughout the body is pooled into the vital organs by the restriction of the capillaries in the extremities. This is because if we are cut or injure our limbs (the things we must use to fight with), we don't bleed to death instantly. Blood loss will be much slower than normal. This pooling of the blood is why we feel light headed or sick to our stomach when afraid for any length of time. Adrenaline is dumped into the system. Adrenaline is super soldier serum. It's like tapping into a power generator. It supercharges your system, making you many times faster, more powerful and more alert than you were a moment ago.

But these physiological changes are unfamiliar to most of us. We seldom get a fear induced adrenal dump on a daily or even monthly basis. To most people, this state of being is unusual and, as such, we view it as foreign and unfriendly when, in fact, it is necessary to our survival. Fear is your ally, not your enemy. We need it. Accept it. Embrace it for you are never more prepared to survive than when you feel the pangs of fear.

COMBATIVE MINDSET

The second aspect of psychological preparation is preparing for hurt or injury. Years ago I developed what is called a survival scale to illustrate this concept. The scale ranges from no damage to hurt, to injury, to death. No damage and death are self explanatory, but hurt and injury are two separate things. Hurt is bruises, contusions, cuts, black eyes, etc. Unlike the movies, don't expect to come out of any physical encounter with anyone without being hurt in some way. We can live with hurt. Injury, on the other hand, is more serious. Injury consists of broken bones, severe cuts, concussion, detached retinas etc. Injury usually requires medical attention. It's important to make such distinctions to be mentally prepared. In any unarmed encounter with an average person, we tell our students that they will be hurt. It is the nature of the beast. Unless you are vastly superior, you're likely to be hurt in some way. You should accept this as fact and prepare for it. When any weapon is injected into the fray, the ante goes up. Now you expect not only to be hurt, but severely injured. You need to accept the fact that you will probably have to go to the hospital as a result of the encounter. In this way, the mind prepares to keep fighting under stress. It helps to ensure that if you are struck, cut or otherwise injured, that you won't freeze and be killed on the spot. By mentally preparing for the worst, you prepare the mind to fight on when the going gets tough. Tell yourself that you won't be beaten, you won't

be stopped and you'll do whatever you must do to survive regardless of the attacker's actions.

KILLER INSTINCT

What would make you kill? More importantly, could you really kill another human being? Could you look into his eyes and drive a knife into his heart and watch the lights go out? Out of machismo, most males would say "no problem" - while secretly wondering if they could really do it when it got right down to it. I can tell you right now from experience that if your answer is "maybe," the real answer is "no." Unless you have an extreme motivator that pushes you over the edge in a time of crisis (like saving the life of a child or loved one), you won't do it when the time comes unless you have conditioned yourself ahead of time.

Man has an innate aversion to killing his own species, especially at close range. In war, most killing is done at a distance where it is more impersonal. Men seldom hesitated to drop bombs, fire mortar shells or cannons, even kill with rifles from across a field. As they moved in closer and it becomes more and more personal, they become less and less capable of the act. Contrary to popular belief, only a small percentage of people did most of the close combat killing in almost every war man has engaged in. So what makes you think you could stare someone in the face and end his life just like that? Most normal people have very normal psychological mechanisms to stop this from happening on a regular basis. We have a conscience.

How, then, do we prepare to deal with violence when we must? How do we strip away these psychological barriers that prevent us from acting when we should? The answer is not a simple one. The first thing we must do is resolve any use of force issues we may have long before the situation ever occurs. Hesitation is often brought about by fear. Fear of the consequences of our actions can play a big role in our inability to act. Knowing when the law, a.k.a. our society, condones the use of force is imperative.

First of all, let it be said clearly that every human being has the right to defend himself from aggression and danger. Defense against predators is natural law. Moreover, you have the right to use any force that is necessary to ensure your safety or the safety of the innocent life of another. That being said, let's get into some specifics.

APPROPRIATE FORCE/DEADLY FORCE

Having understood you have the right to use force in your defense, you must also understand that you don't have the right to retaliation or revenge. In self defense, you must use only that force which will stop the attacker from harming you. No more. Unlike war, if you wound an attacker and he falls to the ground clutching his wound, you don't have the legal or moral right to step in and slit his throat unless you can prove that he was still an immediate lethal threat to your life. The use of deadly force is predicated on the concept of imminent danger. This means that you must be in immediate danger of severe bodily harm, injury or death before you can resort to lethal force. If your attacker stops at any time and flees, you can't shoot him in the back as he runs from you unless he's firing back in your direction.

These concepts apply directly to the knife as a self defense tool. Like the gun, a knife is considered a deadly weapon. You should rarely consider ever drawing and using it unless you would also likely draw and use a firearm in the same situation. If an attacker has a weapon, any weapon, it is advisable to draw a weapon of your own to equalize the odds. If I have any choice in the matter, I'd prefer to escalate the use of force whenever possible. If the attacker breaks a beer bottle and threatens me with it, I'll draw my knife. If he draws a knife, I'll draw a gun. If he draws a gun, I'll pull a grenade. You get the picture. But alas, such fantasies are not always accessible outside of the movies.

If your opponent threatens you with physical force, it is not always legally or morally justified to slice and dice him to shreds. The only exception to this rule is when you face an extreme handicap in force or ability, i.e., the 100 pound woman fighting back against a 250 pound man, or perhaps you are older and/or less physically able to defend yourself by other means. In any case, the use of the edged weapon as a self defense instrument should be confined to life and death scenarios.

Though knives are lethal, killing an attacker is not always the objective in self defense. All you really want to do is survive. For that, you need to incapacitate an attacker, making him incapable of fighting back for at least a few moments so you can flee. With this basic survival goal in mind, the slash is invaluable. It can be delivered quickly whenever an attacker's limbs are within range, and the slash does not expose you to counterattack by having to lunge within the kill zone to penetrate the body cavity. Repeated painful slashes to the hands, forearms, shoulders, neck and face will likely force your attacker to think twice about his actions, giving you the chance to exit quickly.

Whenever a person is cut, it produces a particular form of psychological shock, especially if the cut starts to bleed profusely. A person who is cut and starts to bleed may faint, draw back or even lose confidence and break off the encounter. If you cut your attacker several times and he is not sufficiently upset to reconsider or withdraw, you can be sure you are in for the fight of your life. At this point, you'll probably have to permanently maim or kill him to end the encounter, and you'd be justified to do so if he continued his assault. As you can see from this scenario, using a knife for self defense purposes can bring you to a point where you have to shed all visages of what would be civilized behavior and fight for your life. This is something that not every individual can do easily, and no one can do without some mental preparation. Knife combat is savage, brutal and bloody. People get sliced open and people can die. Unless you are certain you can cope with a primal, savage encounter without hesitation, perhaps you should bypass the knife as a self defense tool. He who hesitates is most certain to end up the loser. In a knife fight, you will be afraid. Anyone who tells you he has been in any serious violent encounter and was not afraid is one of two things; he is either a liar or he is insane. And most people are not insane. Accept your fear. Accept that you will be hurt or injured, but you will not be stopped. The trick is not to die. Deal with it and do what you must to survive.

CHAPTER THIRTEEN

TACTICAL CONCEALMENT

"The first rule of weapons combat is to have one with you."

– Richard Ryan

In the past, most pocket knives were carried in the pocket. They were tools not weapons, and quick access was not an issue. Today, tactical folders are the rage and have all but replaced the old time pocket knife. Now, various clip designs dominate the methods of carry allowing the blade to clip onto the pocket or belt and still remain instantly accessible. But accessible is a relative term. Your attacker may or may not give you the time or distance you need to get to a weapon, regardless of how you carry it. In a sudden attack scenario, the weapon will be a secondary concern as you have to resort to unarmed tactics before accessing it. However, after you punch him in the nose and realize that he has two friends waiting in the wings, getting a weapon out quickly may be important.

TACTICAL CARRY METHODS

The first rule of a knife fight is to have one with you. The second rule is to be able to get to it in a time of need. You can carry the blade anywhere you want to. But some carry methods are better than others. For example, let's say that you choose to carry your folder in your back pocket. No problem, right? You can reach back and get it easily. Under most

conditions that's true, but let's say you're tackled or knocked to the ground with an attacker on top of you. Getting to your knife may be a problem, considering you're sitting on it. You should think of the tactical folder as you would a handgun. Would you carry a handgun in your back pocket or stuffed in your shirt? If you do, your ignorance is showing. Carry the tactical folder where you can get to it quickly in a time of need. If you are right-handed, carry it in your right front pocket. Even if some big ugly thug picks you up in a bear hug, you could still pull it out and bury it in his thigh.

One important note is that you need to know exactly how the specific blade you are carrying is opened when taken from your pocket. Some blades open "blade down," some "blade up". Others are designed exclusively for left-handers. It will make a difference in the exact opening grip and method you use, so take the time to examine and practice drawing and opening the blade you will carry.

QUICK ACCESS

As a professional bodyguard, I carried numerous weapons of all types. But you

Although you can carry the weapon almost anywhere, most of the time the best place to carry a tactical folder is in the front pocket of your dominate hand. This ensures your ability to access it quickly regardless of your position.

Always remember that a weapon is just a tool. Having one with you does not ensure your safety. Even if you carry it in a place where you can get to it quickly, it may not be quick enough.

wouldn't have known it from looking at me. I was a walking arsenal dressed immaculately in a three piece Armani suit or casual jacket and jeans. I could blend in at a cocktail party, business conference or in the casinos at Monte Carlo and you'd never know how many tools of destruction I carried at any given moment. Weapons can be carried in holsters, stuffed in clothing, in the folds of a jacket, held on with rubber bands, tape or Velcro. They can be tucked, stashed, pressed, palmed or otherwise concealed from view and accessed in a single lethal second. From a defensive point of view, never underestimate the ability to hide and conceal weapons by anyone. Always assume your would be attacker has something on his possession other than his hands and feet. From a proactive standpoint, the edged weapon is a small lethal instrument that can be carried easily and drawn in a fraction of a second. It is your choice exactly where you carry your weapons, but make it easy to get to them in virtually any position you find yourself in.

DECEPTIVE CARRY METHODS

You may find yourself in a scenario in which you want to have your weapon in hand, but don't want the attacker to know it. This is called deceptive carry. I have traveled all over the world and have never failed to travel without an edged weapon. There are many places where a firearm will get you a prison sentence or worse, but a steak knife or folder will not even get a second glance. And especially in third world countries, it's better to be safe than sorry. I'd rather have a knife when I need it, and deal with the consequences later.

There are ways to carry a weapon in plain view and not have anyone suspect you have it. The best way is the newspaper method. Let's say your shopping on the streets of

Istanbul. Take your folder, open it and grab a local paper. Throw most of the paper away, except for a few sheets. Fold the sheets over and place the folder near the spine. Grip it normally and casually and go about your business. No one will suspect, fear or block a newspaper and it can be a lethal and sudden surprise if you need it.

Another method is to open the weapon and keep it inside a bag or jacket pocket. This could be a shopping bag or a small piece of travel luggage you carry with you. If you find yourself on the bad side of town or in bad company, you can bring the weapon into place in a heartbeat.

CROSSED ARM CARRY

In law enforcement and firearms training, you're taught to always look at the hands because the hands are what can hold the weapons. If the hands are empty, the opponent does not have immediate access to weapons, right? Wrong. The crossed arm carry method is one of the most deceptive ways to carry a knife. The blade is placed in the arm pit and the hands crossed in front of the chest. The arm itself pinches the blade, and the thumb of the carry hand presses it against the inner triceps. The blade could be closed with a kinetic opening knife. This allows you to remove the fingers of the blade hand and show them to the opponent. This, along with proper body language, creates the illusion that you have no weapons. To use it, raise the defensive arm, grasp the blade and bring it out away from the arm in one swift action.

CROSSED HAND CARRY

Though not as tricky as the crossed arm carry, this method is effective with small knives. The hands are crossed in front of the body with the blade concealed along the forearm of the defensive limb. This method

Police officers and people trained in firearms are taught to look for weapons in the hands. They are told that if you can see the hands, the opponent is not holding a weapon. This is not always true. The cross arm carry is one of the most deceptive concealment methods because the opponent can see both hands, yet the weapon is tucked under the arm and held in place by pressure from the muscles of the upper arm and the chest.

The attacker could even remove his hand, gesture with it and return it to the handle of the blade without your knowing it. In one swift motion he can bring it from under the arm..

...and deliver a sudden attack! Just because you see someone's hands does not mean they don't have immediate access to a weapon. Try it for yourself. Tuck the weapon under the arm with the blade facing the floor. Cross your arms and take a look in the mirror. Can you see the weapon? Can you get to it in a heartbeat?

Another effective method of deceptive carry is the cross hand method. Although this position is slightly more suspicious, it can still effectively hide the blade from view. It is especially good when in a group of other people, during low light conditions or when you are not being scrutinized too harshly. Clasp the blade in any grip and hide it behind the arm. Stay relaxed and try to look casual.

If you need it, the weapon is right in front of you ready to be put directly into action.

It is important to remember to bring the defensive hand high and to the central line with each drawing action, regardless of the method of concealment. This is done to automatically protect the upper body from attack and to ensure that you don't accidentally cut yourself when you draw the weapon.

Although any attack angle is possible from almost any method of carry, it is wise to use the simplest and most direct path to your target. If your hands are down, such as in the cross arm carry, the blade would rise directly into the path of the opponent's attack. Spend some time experimenting with different angles and lines of motion.

is a very casual way to carry the blade and could be used when blending into a crowd or in any situation in which you won't be severely scrutinized.

PALMING METHODS

Any weapon can be "palmed." Palming is the act of placing a weapon in one hand and hiding it with that hand or against the forearm or the leg. This position won't fool anyone who's really paying close attention, but could also be used in a crowd or under low light conditions.

The trick to tactical concealment is to make the position look natural. Most of the information we receive from another person is nonverbal. Often we innately sense whether someone is agitated, excited, uncomfortable or deceptive just by his body language alone. If you feel like you are hiding something, people will sense this, so spend some time practicing accessing and holding your weapons in all the hidden positions. Use a mirror and try to smooth out any problems with stance and positioning. Remember, the advantage to deceptive carry methods is the element of surprise. If your body language alarms the opponent, he will be ready for you and you lose your advantage.

CHAPTER FOURTEEN

REALISTIC TRAINING

"Nothing ever becomes real until it is experienced."

– John Keats

Knowledge is useless unless it is applied. Without specific application, knowledge is just trivia. In application, it becomes fact and experience. You must practice what you know. However, that practice can take many forms. It can be mental, as in the practice of visualization, or physical, as with the repetition of techniques for the improvement of skill. Or it can be both mental and physical, as it is in a sparring match where you must deal with and adapt to the strengths and weaknesses of people and situations.

FORM AND FUNCTION

The art of the blade is a psychophysical skill. Both form and function must be combined for maximum effect. Form is the ability to execute techniques with precision. Function implies that ability to deploy these techniques and tactics with the necessary speed, power, accuracy and timing. It is possible for a person to have great form without the ability to functionally apply it. A person may have good form, as in a slow motion demonstration of techniques, but lack the speed or another ingredient to make it work in real life. It is also possible to have function without form, as in the novice who may be physically gifted but cannot control

those gifts with any effect. For example, a novice may have naturally fast reflexes but becomes wild and ineffective when forced to use them. You need both form and function.

When you practice your techniques, it is advisable to spend the beginning of any practice session working on form. Program the best technique into your bio-computer when you are fresh. The more skill required for an action, the more you want to practice before you move on to more demanding activities. If you wait until the end of the workout, when you're tired, it's likely that you will substitute gross motor skills for finite actions and you could actually regress in skill.

Once you have the form down, add function to your movement progressively. As you work, begin to push the limits of your force matrix, emphasizing, for example, the components of speed and accuracy in your actions. With each repetition push the envelope a little more until you can't push it anymore, and you begin to lose all semblance of form. Then back off and start again with the same or another technique.

How long do you practice? Well, that

depends on you. Most of us have lives that place a great demand on our time and cannot spare more than a few short practice sessions every week. But that's all right because quality of practice is infinitely more important than quantity. You can make your practice sessions short and intense and derive great benefit from them.

SPARRING

Throughout my travels, I have come across all kinds of people from all walks of life. I have had the pleasure of knowing and working with many great and skilled people from many different disciplines. I have tried to learn everything I could from everyone I could. Sometimes this learning process took the form of sparring. I have never failed to learn something valuable from a good sparring match. Even if the opponent knows very little, he can be a great teacher. People who lack formal training are often more creative and instinctive than those bound by a classical style. They fight from instinct,

doing whatever they think they can to survive. This can be of great value in learning to deal with any and all kinds of attacks. On the other hand, those trained in some form of defense offer the experience of dealing with style, tactics and a structured attack. This, too, is of great value. In any case, you should endeavor to spar as many different types of people, as often as you possibly can. Learn from the experience. What did they do well? What were their weaknesses? What could you do against this type of person next time? These experiences and the lessons they teach will serve you well if you ever find yourself in a real life situation.

Then there are the posers. These are people who claim to be experts, but are wholly unwilling to prove it in battle. They tell you they never spar because "their art is too deadly." The martial arts are about fighting, and you've got to fight to learn them. Sure you can learn theory and technique without throwing a single blow. But that's like learning to play chess by only discussing the rules. You can learn the moves, but not their true application. To learn to fight, you must fight. If you are studying some form of martial arts for the art alone, no problem, theorize away. But if your goals are truth, reality and true skill, you have to move from the realm of theory into the world of application.

Since it is illegal (and immoral) to go looking for trouble in order to test your skills, sparring is the best way to learn and hone your abilities. People who say their art is too deadly to spar are full of it. The most deadly art today is the art of combat firearms. If you make one mistake on the range or in a fun house, someone could be dead. Mistakes in firearms training are usually much more deadly than those in martial arts, yet those in the industry still find a way to practice their skills. I have trained numerous S.W.A.T. and special operations teams and we used

Ryan oversees reactive sparring at the world famous Gunsite Firearms Training Center where he designed and implemented their tactical edged weapons program.

simunitions, paintball and even live fire in our training scenarios. This is "sparring with the gun," and it is one of the best forms of training available. Surely if the firearms industry can find a way to spar, any student of the martial arts can find a safe way to practice his skills.

Still I know celebrated self defense instructors who never practice any form of reactive sparring. They demonstrate under controlled conditions, but won't enter into a freestyle situation where they are not in absolute control. Top that off with the fact that many of them have never actually been in a real knock down, drag out fight in their lives, and you've got a really weird paradox. Think about it. Only in the martial arts and related industries do we find teachers that teach a subject but have never actually used what they teach. Would you take lessons from a swimming instructor who has never been in water? In most endeavors doing so would be insane, but not in the martial arts. It's true that you can teach the basics of anything if you have been taught by a competent instructor, but knowledge is one thing and experience is another. There are certain lessons that can only be learned by experience. I believe that the reason some

instructors avoid sparring is fear. Many are afraid that they will perform less than adequately, fearing that their performance will not live up to their reputation or boasts they have made about themselves. Instead of wanting to learn and improve from the experience, they fear it. They will come up with all types of excuses not to spar. "My techniques are too deadly" or "I might accidentally kill you." Whatever. This should send your baloney meter off the scale. Sparring is one of the best teachers you can ever have, and if you don't do it you're missing the whole point. Whether novice or master, if you don't spar you're missing valuable lessons that can only come from this experience.

SPARRING VERSUS FIGHTING

It is important to remember though that sparring is not fighting. Fighting is sudden, savage, brutal and often to the finish. Sparring is a laboratory for you to test your techniques and tactics in a controlled environment against another living, breathing, thinking person. It is a place to sharpen your reactions and hone your timing, and to learn and apply what you know. I try to spar as many different people

as I can, as often as I can, because everyone acts and reacts a little differently. You learn invaluable lessons by having to deal with these people. Sure, it's not real fighting. I know it and they know it (well most do), but that's not the point. The point is that you've got to apply what you know under the most realistic situations you can, and freestyle sparring is one of the best ways to do that. Since I rarely get into a real knife fight on a weekly basis, sparring will have to do.

Now, of course, I never recommend sparing with "live blades" for the same reasons I would never do live fire S.W.A.T. entry scenarios with real people down range. Use your head and use safety equipment. Purchase the best equipment you can and structure the training with built-in safety procedures. Make sure everyone knows the perimeters of action, what they can and cannot do. It's also a good idea to have a first aid kit handy and have a contingency plan should ole Murphy look in on your training.

GENERAL SPARRING CONCEPTS

To the uninitiated, sparring with the blade may seem like a wild exchange of slashes

and stabs. In reality, it involves myriad details and a subtle and intricate interplay of technical ability, reaction time, fighting experience and sometimes a kind of "sixth" sense you need to anticipate an opponent's movements. Knife sparring can be an enlightening experience. Sparring with the blade makes you focus on precision and accuracy and, because it's so very fast, it forces you to maintain absolute concentration. Blink or flinch and you're hit. Because of the speed and focus required, I have used weapons sparring to push the threshold of my reactive abilities and you can do the same. Sparring with weapons, especially the knife, can force your speed and reaction time to its limits and beyond. It can be one of the most productive and exciting exercises in the martial arts.

RULES OF SPARRING

For sparring to be a safe and productive experience, you need to have certain rules of engagement. Everyone should be well versed in what they can and cannot do in a given scenario. Here are a set of guidelines for all involved:

1. Control yourself and your actions. Remember that sparing is not fighting. In

fighting the objective is to cause as much pain and injury as you can in the shortest possible time frame. In sparring, the objective is to learn and improve. You should go all out but refrain from causing any injury or trying to maliciously dominate your opponent.

2. Use protective gear. This is just plain old common sense. Protect yourself with as much gear as the scenario and the environment dictates. For instance, if you are sparring in a school on a matted floor, you can probably wear only minimal equipment. But if you're sparring outside in a parking lot or other location populated with potential dangers, it might be a good idea to put on full contact gear. More gear also allows for more variations in technique. This is my favorite form of sparring, full contact weapons sparring, because anything goes. By wearing protective headgear and using fighting gloves with fingers, you cannot only fight with the blade, but you can interject full contact punches and kicks into the mayhem.

3. Control the environment. For safety reasons, you should make sure the environment is sanitized of anything that could cause severe injury. Don't spar in confined places with glass windows. Someone could be sent flying through one. I know; I've done it. Watch for things someone could trip over or fall upon. Before you spar in a new place, do a 360 degree logistics check to determine any problems with the environment, and don't hesitate to stop the match if someone nears a danger spot.

4. Work your tactics. Don't just throw your favorite techniques. It does you no good if all you do in a sparring match is score with your best strike. Try other techniques. Better yet, try to analyze your

immediate opponent. How fast is he? How much reach does he have or how fast is he on his feet? What are his weaknesses and how can you exploit them? Keep thinking and use everything you have to deal with whomever you face.

5. Learn from your mistakes. Be creative. Find creative solutions to the problems that are presented in this situation. If someone gets to you repeatedly, stop and figure out why. Develop solutions to the problem and return to freestyle sparring. In this way, you are always analyzing and improving your techniques and tactics.

SAFETY AND EQUIPMENT

Like fencing, knife fighting can be a safe endeavor. Moreover, it can be an exciting and invigorating activity. Nothing quite gets the blood pumping as another human being standing in front of you in freestyle combat. The first rule of safety equipment is to have some. It is foolish to cross blades or fists with someone without protection. Unlike fencing, there is no standard for knife fighting equipment. But with a little foresight and ingenuity, it shouldn't be hard to acquire a few pieces that make sparring with the blade safe. If you're serious about it in the first place, you should look into a knife fighting or fencing school. They should be able to provide you with a source for some of the equipment you need. Calling the college athletic department may help also.

HEAD AND FACE PROTECTION

The first things you need are head and face protection. Even with a rubber or false blade, you could take an eye out, or worse. I never spar with weapons without some form of eye and throat protection, and I've been doing it for 20 years. The fencer's helmet is a good choice because of the wire cage and good visibility. If you buy a good one, it will be

One of the more unique aspects of the DCM Tactical Edged Weapons program is the emphasis on realistic training and equipment. Courses feature hands-on work with anatomically correct and lifelike dummies.

Here the instructor is using a dummy arm which allows the student to use live weapons to attack and defend with maximum speed and power. This allows him to perfect his grips, strikes and defenses without fear of harming his training partners.

A hard rubber head helps to create realism in a training session. This head is kept in slight motion, thereby allowing the defender to attack the vital targets with pinpoint accuracy.

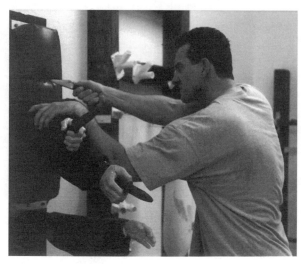

Ryan has also designed numerous pieces of personal training equipment in order to perfect his skills. Here he practices trap and kill techniques with a four-limbed training dummy. It features flexible arms, a spring loaded leg for kicking, and hands capable of holding any weapon.

strong, sturdy and secure, allowing full contact shots to the face and some protection for the throat. If you don't have that, at very least use some form of goggles for the eyes. Most sporting goods stores have sports goggles and some of the equipment used in paintball combat games is also very good.

THE TRAINING KNIVES

I fenced for many years and had a great time. The sport requires lightning fast reactions and is great for eye-hand coordination. However, fencing is not knife fighting. Although they are related, they are like apples and oranges. They're both fruit, but that is where the comparison ends. The technique of the long sword is much different than its short cousin. Other than the obvious

reach factor, the foil or saber may bend on contact. Some of the training knives I've used have failed to be as forgiving. A sparring knife made out of anything other than a relatively soft rubberlike compound can still be dangerous in a full contact scenario. Plastic or aircraft aluminum may be more realistic, but a hard thrust to an unprotected body could be a real problem. Therefore,

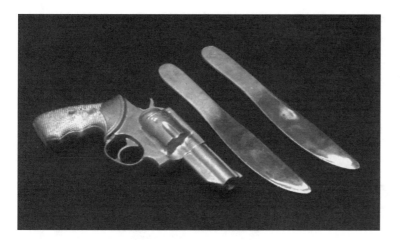

I recommend finding a knife that is sturdy, with a relatively blunt tip that will give with thrusting attacks. Check out your local cutlery shops or catalogs for ideas.

Although not absolutely necessary, I highly recommend some form of forearm and hand protection. With long, drawn out training sessions or matches you will take punishment in these areas. Bruising is common. The best bet is equipment designed for this purpose, but the average sporting goods store has soccer shin guards (the flexible kind) and street hockey gloves that suit this purpose well. Other protective gear may include elbow, knee and shin guards, throat protection and a cup.

CREATIVE SCENARIOS

Sparring should not be confined to a one-on-one scenario. Sparring can be two-on-one for more experience. It should not always be a draw knives and square off situation either. Use your imagination. Move out of the school and into the real world with your sparring scenarios. Work inside and out paying attention to logistics and safety. Work out different situations in which you might be attacked and play each role, attacker and attacked, in turn. Use safety equipment and try to make the scenarios as real as you can.

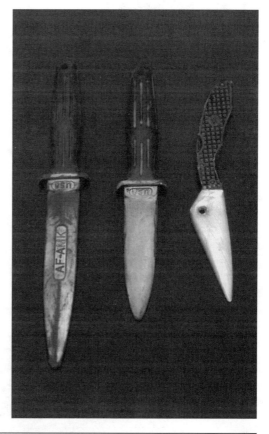

The Legend of the Great Brown Stork

AT A TOP SECRET DOJO...

Welcome to the house of death and destruction. I am supreme grandmaster Sofat. How may I enlighten you?

I have heard you are a great blademaster and I come to see what I can learn. Will you show me your art?

Even though I can see you are pitifully unworthy I will make and attempt to teach you the way of the brown stork...

... can you afford it?

LATER, AFTER RUNNING MY VISA CARD...

Listen carefully... The deadly art of the brown stork comes from the ancient temple of sum dum fool.

In technique number 3,537-B, the blade of the stork is raised high to swoop down on it's unsuspecting prey. The other wing is held high above the head to distract the victim. The knee is raised in the coiled crane position to protect the bladder. A second, more lethal blade is clutched by the toes to attack the spleen... bla... bla... bla...

Really? That's pretty impressive. May I have the honor of sparring with you...

...to see how effective it is?

WHAT?!!? SPARRING !!? You mean actually fighting each other? Are you crazy?! The brown stork technique is too deadly, you'd be killed instantly!

Oh. So if you don't actually spar, how do you know if it really works?

Because I told you so, that's why!

HEY!? Where are you going? Don't you want to take lessons? Wait!

Don't forget to take a catalog...

"Truth cannot be acquired without first experiencing reality."

© Richard Ryan 1998

CHAPTER FIFTEEN

THE FUTURE OF THE BLADE

*"Our scientific power has outrun our spiritual power.
We have guided missiles and misguided men."*

– Martin Luther King, Jr.

We live in a world of racing technology. A complex and intricate society that becomes more and more dependent on computers and micro circuitry everyday. In the last century we have made incredible advances in science and medicine, but our social achievements have not kept pace. Our streets still run rampant with crime. We still shed the blood of our own on a regular basis. Below the surface of our ordered society lies chaos held in check by the threat of our laws and those who try to enforce them. We are still the same old predator, and the most warlike species ever to walk the earth. Until this changes, there will always be a need for the arts of war and a demand for knowledge of martial arts and weaponry.

I thank God we live in a society that allows books such as this to be written. However, if you follow the lessons of the past, it is probable that this grand experiment in freedom will not last, at least in its present form. At no time in history has there been a society as free as ours where men could keep and bear arms without restriction. After all, an armed society is a free society. An armed populous can not only defend itself from crime but from tyranny as well. Freedom is enforced by the threat of force. But despite

hundreds of years of unprecedented freedoms, a dark cloud seems to be slowly descending. Little by little, our freedoms are eroding. Each year more laws and more restrictive gun legislation are proposed. These laws chip away at our basic rights. It isn't going to happen overnight, but it is likely that our right to own firearms will be taken away someday or, at the very least, severely restricted. The good news is that the government will never be able to legislate away martial arts and many other forms of weapons. In the martial arts, your hands and feet are the weapons. A sharp stick or piece of glass becomes a knife, a tree limb a baton or staff. These things you cannot legislate out of existence.

In any case, the right to carry a pocket knife will probably be with us much longer than the right to carry a firearm. Government might be able to legislate away our firearms and ammunition, but never our access to sharp tools and instruments. Even if politicians go so far as to outlaw tactical folders, the edged weapon will still be prevalent in our society. We need knives in daily life and they will always be accessible in one form or another. Because of this, knowledge of the art and science of edged weapons is a practical and important skill set. And one that you should know as part of both your personal rights and your private survival plan. It is my hope that you have learned and benefited from the knowledge in this book. It is your right to have it. But always remember that with great knowledge comes great responsibility. You have the moral obligation not to use what you have learned here unless you have no other option. The responsibility to protect yourself lies with you and you alone. Use it with honor and restraint. Take care and stay safe.

REQUEST

I want your feedback! I am always interested in your comments, suggestions, new techniques and tactics and opinions about what you like and use from my seminars, books and videos. My goal is to provide the most realistic and effective material I can. If a technique or concept doesn't work for you, or is particularly effective, please let me know.

Send your comments and letters to:

Richard Ryan
c/o Tactical Edged Weapons
P.O. Box 54962
Phoenix, Arizona 85078-4962

E-mail me at: edgedweapons@hotmail.com
Or see our web site at:
www.ryandefensesystems.com

THE TERMINOLOGY OF DYNAMIC COMBAT/TACTICAL EDGED WEAPONS

The following is an alphabetical list of some of the terminology used in this book. Many of the words or concepts are unique to the art of Dynamic Combat and were developed especially for this system. Others are simple definitions of terms that are relevant to the art of knife fighting.

ALTERNATIVE STRIKING
The use of unexpected or unconventional strikes in an encounter.

ATTACK ZONE
The most common range in which attacks are launched which is defined as the distance one step out from arms' reach.

BALANCE
A state of equilibrium that allows for maximum use of force and motion.

BALLISTIC WEAPONS
All weapons that are thrown, shot or fired at an adversary.

BIO-COMPUTER
The brain, man's biological computer that governs all thought and action.

BLADE MASTER
A master knife fighter.

BLEEDERS
Body targets designed to open up the circulatory system of the body.

BLOCK
The stopping of in incoming attack force against force.

CENTERLINE
An imaginary line used as a tracking device for you to keep yourself in a position of advantage during a conflict.

CENTERLINE TRACKING
The act of maintaining centerline positioning when in movement.

CENTRAL LINE
An imaginary line running vertically on the body used as a reference point for the attack and defense of the body's vital targets.

CENTERMASS
The largest and most centralized point of weight on an attacker's body.

CONCEALMENT
The act of hiding a weapon from view.

COUNTERATTACK
A term used to describe the act of evading, absorbing or stopping an attack and launching one of your own.

CUT AND RUN
A DCM strategy designed to cut anything you can reach and then move away, keeping as much distance as possible from the attacker.

CUT AND STAY
A DCM strategy designed to stand your ground by necessity or by choice and defend against an attack without retreat.

CUT AND KILL
A DCM strategy designed to attack or force a conclusion to a knife encounter through aggressive action.

DANGER ZONE
The 360 degree area around a defender, defined as two or more steps from the kill zone.

DCM
An acronym for the Dynamic Combat Method.

DEADLY FORCE
Force that is likely to severely injure or kill.

DEFENSE
A collection of techniques and tactics designed to keep one from harm or injury.

DIRECT ATTACK
Any attack that makes no attempt to hide its intentions, but relies on speed and simplicity for effect.

DYNAMIC COMBAT METHOD
A modern martial art system comprised of a unified collection of philosophies, theories, techniques, tactics and strategies created by Richard Ryan and based on his observations about the truth and realities of combat.

EDGED WEAPON
Any object that can be used to cut, puncture of stab the human body.

END RESULT
The first and most important concept of Dynamic Combat that states in a real encounter the only thing that matters is that one achieves his goals. All strategies, techniques and tactics should be geared toward and adaptable to these general goals.

EVASION
The act of avoiding contact with an attacker or his attack through movement of the feet or body.

FIXED BLADE
A single section knife whose handle and blade are fixed in place.

FENCING
The art or practice of attack and defense with the foil or saber.

FLEXIBLE WEAPONS
Any weapon that becomes flexible during its use, designed to whip, strike or catch and trap an opponent's body or weapons.

FOOTWORK
The techniques of foot movement designed to attack and defend effectively.

FORCE MATRIX
The concept in Dynamic Combat that speed, power, accuracy and timing are the four most important components to the use of force in any situation.

IMMOBILIZERS
Attacks with the blade that are designed to render an opponent immobile through the destruction of joints, muscle or connective tissue.

IMPACT WEAPON
Any weapon designed to create a clubbing or bludgeoning force.

INDIRECT ATTACK
All attacks predicated with a fake, feint or a deception of any type.

INSTINCTIVE
Any technique, tactic or maneuver that is based on an impulsive reaction from external stimuli.

KILLER INSTINCT
The ability to ruthlessly use extreme force or finish off an attacker without hesitation.

KILL ZONE
The distance in which an individual can reach out and touch you without having to take a step.

LINE OF FIRE
The exact path that a strike, weapon or bullet travels before impact.

MARTIAL ART
A collection of philosophies, techniques, strategies and tactics designed for war and interpersonal combat.

MINDSET
The state of mind of a fighter that incorporates philosophical and psychological behavioral patterns designed to deal with and function under the extreme stresses of combat.

PARRY
The defection of an incoming blow at a right angle to its trajectory.

QUICKSTEP
Any high speed footwork maneuver designed to cover distance as fast as possible.

RIP CUTS
A cut that enters the body by thrusting and then employs leverage to expand the wound cavity.

REACTION TIME
The time it takes you to recognize and deal with an action by an opponent.

RESPONSE LINE
An imaginary line based on our individual sense of proximity danger, used to control distance in a conflict.

SHIELD
The use of the limbs of the body to cover the vital targets and absorb punishment without serious injury.

SIGHT ALIGNMENT
The alignment of a strike with an opponent's line of vision in order to distort his depth perception.

SLASH
A cut using the edge of the blade in a circular or semicircular fashion.

STAB
A puncture wound created by a piston-like linear use of the blade by injecting the point into the target.

STRATEGY
A general game plan designed to meet the enemy under advantageous conditions.

TACTICAL FOLDER
A modern folding knife designed in part as a defensive tool and weapon.

TACTICS
The deployment of specific individual techniques and maneuvers designed to gain an advantage in a conflict.

TIME DISTANCE VARIABLE
The concept that the greater distance you are from an opponent, the greater your reaction time and vice versa.

TEW
An acronym for Tactical Edged Weapons, the knife fighting system created by Richard Ryan and derived from the art of Dynamic Combat.

TRAP
A temporary immobilization of a limb or weapon designed to pave the way for an attack.

USP
An acronym for the Universal Striking Pattern. The USP is an imaginary geometrical pattern of movements that represents common lines of attack and defense in a three dimensional plane.

ABOUT THE AUTHOR

Richard Ryan is one of the nation's leading authorities on martial arts, self-defense and tactical weapons training. His programs represent a lifetime of research and development, with the singular focus on practical application in real-life situations. Mr. Ryan is a longtime advocate of the scientific approach to self-defense and his methods are characterized by their realism, effectiveness and the ease at which they can be learned and applied. Recognized as an innovator and master of hand-to-hand and weapons combat, he has designed and implemented unique tactical survival programs for numerous S.W.A.T., special operations teams and law enforcement agencies. A former professional bodyguard, Gunsite Firearms Training Center Instructor and U.S. Marksmanship Academy Instructor, Mr. Ryan has vast experience in all areas of personal protection and is renowned for his comprehensive knowledge of martial arts, firearms and self-defense.

The Dynamic Combat Method is the innovative, exceedingly effective fighting art that Mr. Ryan invented and has refined over the past 20 years. It forms the foundation for his teaching. A comprehensive personal survival system, Dynamic Combat addresses all aspects of violent confrontation, including an in-depth study of all forms of weapons craft. He has developed unique insights into the practical use of almost every weapon, from the simple pen or pencil to the tactical assault rifle. He is also the creator of the highly acclaimed Tactical Edged Weapons System, the subject of this book.

Richard Ryan is a gifted athlete, artist, inventor and writer. His exceptional teaching skills have been appreciated by his many longtime students, law enforcement and government operatives, and those thousands of people who have attended his very popular seminars over the years. His dedicated and meticulous search for the fundamental truths of self-defense have been an integral part of providing insights into an area of human experience that is often shrouded in mystery and misconception.

Mr. Ryan and his company, RDS International, offer a wide variety of services to government, law enforcement and qualified civilians. The success of his programs can be attributed to his cutting edge innovations and his sensible approach to the use of force and individual personal safety. His presentations, books and videos are brutally honest, direct and highly enlightening, and continue to provide answers for those touched by violence or in the line of fire.

19.05